THE RESONANT MARKET SERIES

The Conscious Flow of Markets

Perception, Probability, and Conscious Decision-Making in Financial Markets

Deepanshu Suman

2025 First Edition

Copyright

Title: The Conscious Flow of Markets
Author: Deepanshu Suman

First Edition
ISBN: 978-93-344-5226-6

Disclaimer: This book is intended for educational, conceptual, and professional reflection on financial markets, decision-making, and probabilistic frameworks. The content does not constitute professional financial, investment, or legal advice. Readers should exercise independent judgment and consult qualified professionals before applying any ideas presented in this work.

Dedication

To all the traders, thinkers, and seekers who strive to understand the unseen patterns of markets,
To those who embrace uncertainty with curiosity and courage,
And to the minds that seek alignment between awareness, probability, and action this book is for you.

Preface

Financial markets are not mere machines of numbers and charts they are living systems, shaped by perception, awareness, and collective cognition. Behind every price movement lies the influence of human consciousness: emotions, intentions, and probabilistic expectations interact to create outcomes that defy purely deterministic explanations. This book exists to bridge the gap between traditional market analysis and a deeper, more holistic understanding, integrating **consciousness, behavioral finance, probabilistic thinking, and decision theory** into a practical and reflective framework.

As the third installment in *The Resonant Markets Series*, this book completes a conceptual journey:

- **Book 1: Decoding the Human Nature of Market Moves** explored the role of *emotion* in shaping market behavior.
- **Book 2: The Market's Hidden Frequency** examined *resonance* the alignment between trader psychology and market dynamics.
- **Book 3: The Conscious Flow of Markets** investigates the *conscious flow* of markets, showing how awareness, perception, and intentionality influence probabilistic outcomes.

Target Audience: This book is designed for:

- Advanced retail and professional traders seeking conceptual and psychological mastery.
- Readers interested in behavioral finance, decision theory, and mindfulness in trading.
- Followers of *The Mind of Markets* series seeking deeper philosophical and practical insight.
- AI- and quant-inspired traders and analysts looking for intuitive, probability based decision frameworks.

Core Objectives:

- Illuminate how market movements emerge from *perceptual probabilities* rather than fixed cause-effect dynamics.

- Introduce *quantum-inspired frameworks* for decision-making under uncertainty.
- Offer practical exercises for *awareness, probability visualization, and emotional calibration.*
- Integrate conceptual mastery with actionable trading tools, making philosophy applicable in real-world markets.

Purpose and Unique Value:

- Explores financial markets as *probabilistic, consciousness-influenced systems*, shaped by perception, awareness, and collective cognition.
- Bridges behavioral finance, quantum-inspired decision theory, and mindfulness, providing frameworks that unify rational probability with intuitive awareness.
- Provides actionable mental models, exercises, and reflective practices for traders to align perception, probability, and emotional flow.

Readers are invited to engage actively with this work: to observe, reflect, journal, and experiment with conscious decision-making. By doing so, you will not only develop a deeper understanding of markets but also cultivate a mindset capable of navigating uncertainty with clarity, adaptability, and insight.

Introduction

Financial markets are often viewed as predictable systems machines governed by supply, demand, and fundamental metrics. Yet anyone who has traded or invested knows that markets rarely behave in a fully deterministic manner. Prices move in ways that defy logic, trends shift unexpectedly, and volatility appears without warning. These phenomena emerge not just from external events, but from the interplay of **human perception, awareness, and collective cognition**.

Markets as Probabilistic, Perception-Dependent Systems

Markets are best understood as **probabilistic systems**, where outcomes are distributed across a spectrum of possibilities rather than fixed results. Every participant observes, interprets, and reacts to the market through the lens of their own perception, biases, and knowledge. In this sense, **price movements are reflections of collective probability waves**, continuously shaped by the awareness and decisions of traders, investors, and institutions.

This perspective reframes markets from deterministic machines into **dynamic, perception-driven systems**. Probabilities collapse into actual outcomes when participants act similar to the observer effect in quantum systems. Understanding this probabilistic nature allows traders to navigate uncertainty with insight, rather than being surprised by it.

Why Traditional Analysis Is Insufficient

Traditional trading analysis technical patterns, fundamental metrics, and historical correlations assumes a level of predictability that often does not exist. Without **awareness, emotional calibration, and reflective perception**, even the most sophisticated strategies can fail. Human emotions like fear, greed, and hope distort probability assessments, creating gaps between expected and actual market behavior.

Recognizing markets as **conscious-influenced, probabilistic systems** shifts the focus from predicting fixed outcomes to **aligning perception,**

awareness, and action. Traders who integrate probabilistic thinking and emotional calibration gain an edge by seeing opportunities and risks more clearly and responding with intentionality.

How to Use This Book

This book is designed to be **interactive and reflective**, not merely informational. Readers are encouraged to actively engage with the material through:

- **Reflection:** Pause to consider how your perception, biases, and emotional state influence your interpretation of market movements.
- **Journaling:** Maintain a trading or decision journal to track observations, thought processes, and insights over time.
- **Probability Visualization:** Use the exercises to map potential outcomes and understand the probabilistic nature of trades and market events.

By actively practicing these methods, you will cultivate a deeper awareness of both the **market environment and your own decision-making processes**, laying the foundation for conscious, probability-driven trading mastery.

In the chapters that follow, we will explore **markets as probabilistic systems**, the role of the trader's conscious mind, and frameworks for integrating awareness, probability, and emotional flow into actionable strategies. Together, these tools and insights will help you navigate uncertainty with clarity, confidence, and conscious alignment.

Contents

Part I

Markets as Probabilistic Systems

Chapter 1

The Quantum Perspective of Markets

Financial markets are not fixed, deterministic systems; they are dynamic environments where countless decisions, perceptions, and interactions converge to produce outcomes that are inherently uncertain. Just as quantum systems in physics exist in a spectrum of possibilities until observed, market prices reflect a probabilistic range of potential outcomes rather than a single, pre-determined value. Understanding markets through this lens requires recognizing that **uncertainty, observation, and awareness** are not just peripheral factors they are integral to how price and probability emerge. In this chapter, we explore the quantum perspective of markets, examining how probabilistic thinking, superposition, and the observer's influence reshape the way we conceptualize trading and decision-making.

1.1 Uncertainty and Superposition in Trading

Markets are fundamentally uncertain. Despite the wealth of data, sophisticated models, and high-speed algorithms, no trader individual or institutional can predict prices with absolute certainty. Rather than viewing this uncertainty as a limitation, advanced traders can embrace it as the **essential fabric of market reality**, a space where probabilistic thinking and conscious awareness converge.

The Nature of Uncertainty in Markets

Every market participant operates with **partial knowledge**. News, earnings reports, macroeconomic indicators, and technical patterns provide signals, but none can fully describe the intricate web of interactions that determine price movements. Each trader's perception is influenced by:

- Incomplete or delayed information.
- Cognitive biases and emotional states.
- Anticipated behavior of other traders, institutions, and algorithms.

This creates an environment of **intrinsic uncertainty**, where outcomes exist not as fixed points but as ranges of probability. Accepting this uncertainty is the first step toward conscious, probabilistic trading.

Superposition: Holding Multiple Possibilities

Borrowing from quantum theory, **superposition** describes the idea that multiple states can coexist until observed or measured. In trading, this concept translates into the mental ability to **hold multiple potential outcomes simultaneously** without prematurely collapsing possibilities into a single expectation.

Analogy: Schrödinger's Trade Imagine considering a trade that could result in profit or loss. In a deterministic mindset, you might fixate on one outcome: "This trade will succeed." In a superposition mindset, you acknowledge both potentialities concurrently: "This trade could gain, lose, or fluctuate within a range of outcomes." Only after you place the trade and observe market behavior does the "state" collapse into a realized result.

This mindset transforms trading from **reactive speculation** into **conscious engagement**, where probabilities guide action rather than certainty dictating it.

Why Superposition Matters for Traders

1. **Reduces Emotional Bias:** By holding multiple outcomes in mind, traders avoid attachment to a single forecast, mitigating fear, greed, and overconfidence. 2. **Improves Risk Management:** Superposition encourages planning for a spectrum of scenarios, making position sizing and stop-loss placement more aligned with reality. 3. **Enhances Adaptability:** Traders attuned to multiple potential outcomes can pivot quickly as market information evolves, rather than being locked into a rigid plan.

Exercises to Cultivate Superpositional Thinking

1. **Outcome Mapping:** For every trade, write down all plausible scenarios, from most likely to extreme cases. Visualize each scenario unfolding simultaneously, and consider your response to each.

2. **Probability Weighting:** Assign subjective probabilities to each outcome. Reflect on how your probabilities change with new information or shifting market conditions.

3. **Decision Superposition Journaling:** Record moments when you feel compelled to commit to a single outcome prematurely. Reflect on how embracing superposition could have altered your choices or emotional response.

Narrative Insight: Trading as a Quantum Experience

Consider a high-frequency trading desk. Algorithms execute thousands of orders per second, each responding to micro-changes in price and liquidity. No single model predicts every outcome; the desk operates on **probability distributions**, constantly updating based on observed market behavior. Traders who step back and observe consciously, rather than reacting impulsively, can **sense patterns in probabilistic waves**, understanding that each decision is an interaction with a cloud of potentialities rather than a march toward a predetermined outcome.

Practical Applications

1. **Dynamic Positioning:** Avoid all-or-nothing bets. Use superpositional thinking to scale into positions gradually, responding to market feedback. 2. **Scenario-Based Stops and Limits:** Instead of fixed stop-losses, consider conditional strategies aligned with multiple possible outcomes. 3. **Reflective Observation:** Allocate periods for non-trading observation, noticing how market probabilities shift, and how perception and bias influence interpretation.

Philosophical Reflection

Embracing uncertainty and superposition invites humility and depth. It teaches traders that **control is partial, and knowledge is probabilistic**, but within this openness lies clarity and power. The market is no longer a rigid system to be conquered, but a living, evolving mirror of collective perception and action. The trader's mind, when trained in probabilistic superposition, becomes an instrument capable of perceiving subtle shifts, anticipating waves of probability, and acting with intention rather than compulsion.

Key Takeaways

- Market uncertainty is intrinsic; it is not a flaw to be eliminated but a reality to be embraced.
- Superposition the ability to hold multiple outcomes simultaneously enhances flexibility, emotional regulation, and strategic clarity.
- Conscious observation and reflection allow traders to navigate probabilistic landscapes skillfully, aligning perception, probability, and decision-making.

- By integrating uncertainty and superpositional thinking, trading becomes a **participatory practice**, where awareness shapes outcomes as much as action does.

Ultimately, **superposition transforms uncertainty from a source of fear into a lens of opportunity**, empowering traders to operate not merely as analysts, but as conscious participants in a dynamic, probabilistic market ecosystem.

1.2 Observation, Awareness, and Market Influence

Every price tick, every order, every shift in market sentiment is, at its core, a reflection of perception. The market is not a mechanical, isolated system; it is a living network of **human attention, expectation, and action**. To engage skillfully with markets, traders must cultivate not just analytical ability, but **deep observation and conscious awareness**. Observation alone is insufficient if unaccompanied by awareness; awareness alone is incomplete if it fails to translate into aligned action. The interplay of these elements observation, awareness, and influence is the foundation of conscious trading.

The Power of Observation

Observation is more than passively watching charts or monitoring indicators. It is the deliberate, focused act of perceiving **patterns, tendencies, and shifts** without the filter of preconception. True observation requires:

- **Non-attachment:** Seeing price movement without immediate judgment or emotional reaction.
- **Detail sensitivity:** Noticing subtle divergences, micro-trends, and behavioral cues in the market.
- **Contextual awareness:** Understanding the broader ecosystem macro news, liquidity flows, and participant psychology.

Analogy: The Watchful Gardener Consider a gardener tending to a diverse ecosystem of plants. The gardener observes the soil, sunlight, moisture, and growth patterns without forcing outcomes. By noticing subtle changes, the gardener intervenes appropriately pruning, watering, or adjusting conditions. Similarly, traders who cultivate **observational awareness** perceive emerging market conditions before taking deliberate, measured action.

Awareness: The Conscious Lens

Awareness builds upon observation. It is the capacity to **perceive not only what is happening, but how you are perceiving it**. Awareness reveals cognitive biases, emotional triggers, and habitual patterns that shape your interpretation of market events.

- **Cognitive Awareness:** Recognize when your mental models are influencing perception more than actual market behavior.
- **Emotional Awareness:** Notice fear, greed, or overconfidence as they arise, and understand their impact on decision-making.
- **Probabilistic Awareness:** Sense the spectrum of potential outcomes, rather than fixating on a single expected price.

Practical Exercise: Mindful Observation Session 1. Set aside a 30–60 minute trading session purely for observation no orders, no trades. 2. Record every market movement that catches your attention. Note your initial interpretations and emotional responses. 3. Reflect on how your biases or assumptions colored your observations. 4. Revisit the same market period after some time to see if your understanding evolved.

Through repeated practice, awareness becomes a **lens for probabilistic perception**, allowing traders to see the market as a dynamic, perception-driven system.

Market Influence: The Observer Effect in Trading

In quantum physics, observation itself affects the system observed. In trading, the principle is analogous: **conscious, informed observation and deliberate action influence market dynamics**. A trader's decisions especially when aggregated with others' can nudge probabilities, shift sentiment, and even create trends. The market is not merely external; it responds to **the attention and intention of participants**.

Analogy: The Stone and the Water Dropping a stone into a calm pond creates ripples that spread outward. Your trades and decisions are like that stone: they interact with the liquidity, sentiment, and collective attention of other participants, creating waves that influence outcomes. Understanding this effect allows you to act with both humility and responsibility.

Actionable Practices to Enhance Influence

1. **Conscious Trade Planning:** Before executing a trade, visualize its impact on the market. Consider how your position size, timing, and strategy might interact with broader flows.

2. **Reflective Journaling:** After each session, record observations of your awareness, emotional state, and the perceived influence of your actions. Over time, this reveals patterns in perception and decision-making.

3. **Adaptive Observation:** Regularly recalibrate your mental models in response to observed market behavior, staying attuned to evolving probabilities.

4. **Meditative Mindset Exercises:** Short mindfulness sessions before trading enhance attentional clarity, allowing for more accurate observation and measured influence.

Narrative Insight: The Conscious Trader as Observer and Participant

Imagine a trader who has mastered observation and awareness. They notice subtle divergences between price action and market sentiment, detect early signs of liquidity shifts, and remain emotionally unhooked from outcomes. When they act, each decision is **deliberate, informed, and probabilistically aligned**. Their trades do not merely react to the market; they interact with the flow, nudging probabilities, creating coherent influence, and aligning personal intention with systemic dynamics.

Reflective Insight

Observation and awareness transform trading from a reactive, anxiety-driven pursuit into a **participatory, conscious practice**. Traders learn to:

- Perceive markets as a **dynamic network of possibilities**, rather than static charts.
- Align perception, probability, and decision-making in real-time.
- Exercise influence responsibly, understanding that attention, action, and intention shape outcomes.

Ultimately, the market is a mirror of collective cognition. By cultivating **observation and awareness**, traders engage not just with price, but with the **probabilistic flow of perception itself**, transforming uncertainty into a medium for conscious action and strategic mastery.

Chapter 2

Probability Clouds and Market States

Markets are not lines they are clouds.

Every price, every tick, every candle we see on a chart is just a single outcome among countless possibilities that could have emerged. Beneath the surface of every movement lies an invisible field of probabilities constantly shifting, colliding, and collapsing as traders make decisions. To understand markets deeply is to stop asking *"What will happen?"* and begin asking *"What could happen and with what likelihood?"*

This chapter invites you into that mindset the probabilistic lens through which great traders view uncertainty. It's not merely about calculating odds; it's about *living with them consciously.*

In deterministic thinking, we look for cause and effect a news event leads to a price jump, a breakout signals continuation, a moving average crossover predicts reversal. It feels comforting, even rational. But markets are not deterministic systems. They are nonlinear, adaptive, and reflexive a vast web of interacting expectations. A single decision by a large participant can shift the entire probability landscape. What was likely a few minutes ago becomes improbable the next.

Imagine the market as a *quantum fog* of potential price paths. Each trade, each choice by a participant small or large slightly alters the density of that fog. Some paths thicken with probability; others fade. When traders act, they are like observers in quantum physics collapsing that fog into a temporary reality: a price print, a tick on the screen.

But immediately, the fog reforms. New data, new emotions, new orders and the cloud of probabilities reshapes again.

This is the essence of trading awareness: not prediction, but participation in a field of evolving probabilities.

2.1 Visualizing Market Possibilities

When most traders look at a chart, they see a story that has already been written a sequence of price bars, candles, or patterns that feel conclusive in retrospect. But a trader operating at a higher level sees something else entirely: a field of *possibilities*, each vibrating with potential energy, waiting to be realized or dismissed by collective human decision.

The chart, in this sense, is not a picture of the past it is a dynamic mirror of what the market believes is possible *now*. Every tick is a new probability update. Every pattern is a temporary snapshot of collective perception, constantly rewritten as new information flows into the system.

This is the true challenge and beauty of trading: to learn to see the invisible structure beneath the visible price. To sense, intuitively and analytically, where possibility thickens where the next high-probability outcome is forming, even before it appears.

—

The Map Beneath the Map

Imagine the market not as a flat line of prices, but as a *probability landscape*. Peaks represent regions of high expectation where market participants believe the price is likely to move. Valleys represent neglect areas few expect the price to reach.

A skilled trader learns to navigate this terrain. They do not merely react to what has happened; they visualize what *could* happen next and assign weight probability to each possible path.

This is the essence of market intuition: not prediction, but **probabilistic imagination**.

> The amateur sees one future; the professional holds many futures in mind, each with a different weight.

When you visualize markets in this way, uncertainty ceases to feel like chaos. It becomes a structured field one that can be mapped, sensed, and adapted to. This shift in visualization transforms your emotional relationship to trading. You move from being surprised by outcomes to dancing with possibilities.

—

Example: The Trader as a Quantum Observer

Consider a simple example: a currency pair hovering around a major resistance level. Most traders see two obvious outcomes a breakout or a rejection. But a more advanced trader sees a spectrum of outcomes, each with a shifting probability based on time, volume, volatility, and sentiment.

- A *clean breakout* with strong volume (40% probability)

- A *fake-out* followed by a swift retracement (30% probability)
- A *slow consolidation* creating indecision (20% probability)
- A *volatility spike* driven by unexpected macro news (10% probability)

None of these are certainties. They are *quantum states* of the market superimposed until reality selects one through the collective observation and action of traders.

And crucially: your *own decision* to enter or wait changes this field. Just as an observer in quantum physics collapses a wave function by measuring it, your orders and those of millions of others change the market's probability cloud.

In trading, you are never outside the system. You are a participant shaping the probabilities you observe.

—

Visualization as Conscious Practice

Visualization in trading is often misunderstood as mere imagination a kind of daydreaming about profit targets and perfect entries. But the visualization we speak of here is deeper it is *probabilistic awareness in motion.*

It means training your mind to:

1. See not one outcome, but many.
2. Feel the weight of those outcomes which are growing stronger, which are fading.
3. Place yourself within that evolving field and act in alignment with it.

You can develop this awareness both analytically and intuitively.

Analytical Visualization Build your probability map through data. Backtest scenarios. Model volatility. Note where liquidity tends to cluster. Your chart becomes not a fixed canvas, but a *heatmap of expectations.*

When you overlay volume profiles, option open interest, or volatility skews, you are effectively visualizing the collective probabilities that other traders have already priced in.

Intuitive Visualization Beyond data, there is resonance. You begin to sense market tone the emotional temperature of the participants. The tape feels "heavy" or "thin," ranges tighten before they explode, and your perception of rhythm sharpens. This is not superstition it's the subconscious integrating countless signals into a felt understanding.

Advanced traders use both: Data informs, intuition integrates.

—

Practical Reflection: The Probability Canvas

Try this exercise next time you prepare for a trade:

1. **Open a fresh chart.** Before drawing lines or indicators, pause. Ask yourself: *What are the 3–5 possible paths from here?*
2. **Assign probabilities.** Don't seek accuracy seek clarity. Which scenario feels most probable, and why? What assumptions drive that feeling?
3. **Sketch them mentally or on paper.** Imagine each path as a curve with its own color and thickness the thicker the line, the higher the likelihood.
4. **Ask: what would change this map?** What news event, volume spike, or sentiment shift would alter the landscape?
5. **Trade only within your map.** If price action begins to align with one scenario, act with conviction. If it deviates, update your probabilities don't defend your bias.

Over time, you'll notice something extraordinary: You stop reacting to single candles or emotional impulses. You begin to think in *distributions*, not certainties. Your trades become calmer, cleaner, more adaptive.

—

The Mirror of Mind and Market

Markets are mirrors of collective consciousness. Every belief, fear, and hope leaves its fingerprint on price. To visualize market possibilities is to see this collective mind in motion to witness the ongoing negotiation between optimism and fear, greed and patience, illusion and truth.

And just as the market's state changes, so does your own internal state. The clearer your awareness, the clearer your probability map. The more reactive your emotions, the more distorted your visualization becomes.

> "You cannot see probabilities clearly when your mind is turbulent because the turbulence is part of the market you are trying to observe."

In this way, trading becomes a practice of consciousness itself. You learn to see, feel, and act within probability clouds not from fear or hope, but from awareness and adaptability. This is the path from reactive trading to mindful mastery.

2.2 Probability Distributions vs Deterministic Thinking

At the core of market misunderstanding lies one dangerous illusion the illusion of certainty. Traders, analysts, even entire institutions often fall into the trap of deterministic thinking: the belief that for every cause, there exists a predictable, linear effect. A rate cut should push equities higher. Strong earnings should lift a stock. Inflation data should weaken bonds.

But markets, alive with perception and expectation, rarely follow these tidy rules. They are not machines; they are consciousness fields self-referential systems shaped by how billions of minds interpret new information in real time.

When you think deterministically, you build brittle models models that shatter under the pressure of real uncertainty. When you think probabilistically, you build flexible maps maps that can bend, adapt, and survive.

—

The Fallacy of Certainty

Deterministic thinking is emotionally seductive. It promises control. It allows us to believe that if we study hard enough, analyze deeply enough, or find the perfect indicator, we can eliminate uncertainty.

Yet the moment we demand certainty from markets, we begin to suffer. Because markets are not puzzles to be solved; they are mirrors reflecting evolving collective psychology.

Every piece of data is not an instruction it is an influence. Every pattern is not a prophecy it is a probability.

To demand certainty from markets is like demanding that the ocean stay still while we surf.

A trader who understands this stops seeking perfect predictions and starts practicing fluid adaptation.

—

Distributions: The Language of Reality

The true language of markets is not cause and effect it is probability distribution. A price at any given moment represents not a fixed truth, but the current *weighted average of all collective expectations.*

Think of the market as a constantly updating probability cloud. Every news event, every trade, every shift in sentiment subtly reshapes this cloud thickening some areas of potential (more likely outcomes) while thinning others (less likely ones).

For example, when inflation data comes in higher than expected, the deterministic thinker says:

> "Rates will rise, so stocks must fall."

But the probabilistic thinker asks:

> "What portion of this data was already priced in? How might this shift the distribution of expectations?"

Maybe the market had already anticipated the bad data. Maybe the reaction is muted because liquidity is thin, or because market participants are waiting for confirmation from the next Fed statement.

The deterministic mind sees one path. The probabilistic mind sees many each with its own weight, velocity, and emotional charge.

—

From Prediction to Probability Mapping

When you stop predicting and start mapping, your relationship to the market changes entirely.

The deterministic trader asks:

> "Will the market go up or down?"

The probabilistic trader asks:

> "What are the possible paths from here, and how is their probability shifting in real time?"

This shift sounds subtle, but it changes everything your emotional posture, your position sizing, your patience, and your ability to perceive risk.

The deterministic trader oscillates between hope and fear. They feel wrong when the market does not follow their plan. The probabilistic trader stays present. They are never entirely wrong only recalibrating.

Their ego is not attached to a single outcome; it is attuned to the fluid geometry of changing odds.

—

Analogy: The Chessboard and the Weather

Deterministic thinking treats the market like chess a closed system where all information is known, and outcomes are theoretically calculable with perfect reasoning.

But markets are not chess; they are more like weather systems.

In chess, you can plan ten moves ahead because nothing external interferes. In markets, there are trillions of interacting variables: central banks, algorithms, geopolitical tensions, investor emotions, liquidity shifts, and the sheer randomness of human behavior.

A meteorologist cannot tell you if it will rain exactly at 3:17 PM next Thursday, but they can tell you there's a 70% chance of rain that afternoon. The skilled trader does the same forecasting probability ranges rather than certainties.

This does not make them vague; it makes them *adaptive*. They navigate volatility not with conviction, but with calibration.

—

Practical Reflection: Thinking in Distributions

To train your mind in probabilistic thinking, try this daily visualization exercise:

1. **Before entering any trade**, list at least three possible outcomes: favorable, neutral, and adverse. Assign a probability to each based on your analysis and intuition.
2. **Journal your reasoning.** What factors led you to these probabilities? What would need to change in price, sentiment, or volume for your probabilities to shift?
3. **As the trade evolves**, update your distribution. Notice when your emotional state tempts you to ignore low-probability but high-impact outcomes.
4. **After exit**, reflect on whether your probability weights matched reality. Over time, you will develop a more accurate sense of how your mind interprets uncertainty.

The goal is not to find the perfect probability it is to strengthen your ability to think in probabilities at all. This is how you build mental resilience. The market no longer feels chaotic; it becomes a dynamic dialogue between your evolving perception and the world's collective reaction.

—

The Psychology of Determinism

Deterministic thinking is not just intellectual it is emotional. It arises from our biological craving for control and closure. The human brain finds randomness uncomfortable. It wants cause, narrative, and certainty because uncertainty feels like danger.

That is why deterministic traders often overtrade or refuse to exit losing positions. They are not trading the market; they are trading their own need to feel right.

To move into probabilistic consciousness, you must become comfortable with ambiguity. This is not resignation; it is mastery. It is learning to act decisively without demanding certainty.

> "Confidence does not come from knowing the future; it comes from knowing how to respond to whatever the future brings."

—

Bridging the Two Worlds

There is, however, a paradox worth noting. Even though markets are probabilistic, deterministic tools still have value but only when used consciously.

Technical patterns, fundamental catalysts, and quantitative models each highlight *local zones of probability.* They are useful not as predictors, but as *probability indicators.* The danger lies not in using them, but in mistaking them for truth.

A deterministic chartist sees a head-and-shoulders and assumes a breakdown is inevitable. A probabilistic trader sees it as a structure that *increases* the likelihood of distribution but also remains open to the possibility of failure and false breakouts.

Thus, the mature trader integrates both:

- Deterministic frameworks as maps of potential.
- Probabilistic awareness as the compass of reality.

—

Exercise: The Spectrum of Belief

Try this experiment for a week:

1. Each morning, write down your directional bias for three markets (for example: EUR/USD, NASDAQ, and Gold).
2. Assign a probability weight to each scenario: bullish, bearish, and neutral.
3. During the day, track how your conviction fluctuates with price action. Note when you start to believe "it must go up" that's determinism creeping in.
4. Each evening, record what actually happened and how your emotional certainty affected your decision-making.

Over time, you'll begin to notice patterns not just in the market, but in yourself. You'll see how quickly the mind clings to singular outcomes, how fear narrows perspective, and how awareness restores flexibility.

—

The Art of Probabilistic Presence

Ultimately, trading is not about predicting it is about participating. The trader's role is not to command the market, but to dance with it to sense the rhythm of probabilities and adjust as the tempo changes.

The shift from deterministic to probabilistic thinking is the shift from ego to awareness. From needing to be right, to needing to perceive clearly. From chasing certainty, to cultivating conscious adaptability.

Markets do not reward certainty; they reward fluid awareness.

When you begin to live this truth, you no longer see markets as adversaries or puzzles. You see them as living expressions of collective probability clouds of potential constantly forming, dissolving, and reforming through human perception and action.

To think probabilistically, then, is not merely a trading skill it is a way of seeing. A deeper consciousness of how uncertainty unfolds not as a threat, but as the very fabric of opportunity.

2.3 How Trader Decisions Collapse Probabilities

In the world of quantum mechanics, a particle exists in a superposition of many possible states until it is observed. The act of measurement doesn't merely reveal the state it defines it. The same principle applies, metaphorically, to markets.

Before a trader acts, price exists as a cloud of probabilities a living, breathing field of potential outcomes shaped by news, sentiment, liquidity, and expectations. Once a trade is placed once capital and conviction meet the wave collapses. The "possible" becomes "actual."

The market, in this sense, is not a deterministic system waiting to be decoded. It's a probabilistic mirror, waiting for observation and participation to define its next move.

From Possibility to Reality

Imagine a stock that could rise, fall, or stay flat after an earnings announcement. Before the release, the market's implied volatility represents this distribution of outcomes. Traders buy calls, puts, and straddles, forming a collective probability cloud. But the moment earnings are announced numbers hit the screen the market reacts. Prices gap up or down, options reprice instantly, and probabilities vanish into a single historical reality.

This process mirrors what physicists call the "collapse of the wavefunction." The collective expectations, once dispersed across many possible futures, converge into one observed state. Every tick, every trade, every decision by a participant adds to this ongoing collapse of uncertainty into the present moment.

Decision as Measurement

Every trader measures the market in their own way through charts, models, gut feeling, or algorithmic logic. These measurements are not passive; they shape behavior, influence liquidity, and feed into the very system they aim to interpret.

When you decide to enter a trade, you collapse your personal probability distribution into a position. You take a stand on what you believe will materialize. The risk and reward you face are simply the mathematical echoes of that collapse. You are both the observer and the participant. The market you experience is not independent of your perception it's entangled with it.

For advanced traders, this understanding reframes the act of trading. It's not just prediction it's participation in a probabilistic field that's constantly being reshaped by collective awareness.

Collective Collapses: The Market as Consensus Reality

Markets are crowds of collapsing probabilities. Each trader's belief each position nudges the aggregate distribution of future prices. When enough capital aligns behind a shared conviction, probability shifts into trend. Momentum, in this view, is not just technical it's psychological inertia.

Consider a rumor about a central bank rate cut. At first, it's one of many possibilities within the market cloud. But as traders start pricing it in buying bonds, selling currencies, shifting portfolios the probability of that outcome begins to dominate. By the time the central bank confirms the move, the market has already collapsed that probability. The "news" becomes redundant; it's been traded into existence.

This is why markets often react counterintuitively why good news can cause prices to fall. The probability was already collapsed in advance, leaving no uncertainty to resolve.

The Trader's Role in Shaping Reality

Trading is not the art of predicting the future it's the art of interacting with probability. You are not merely guessing where prices will go. You are engaging with uncertainty, collapsing one potential future through your decisions and risk management.

The deeper you understand this, the more conscious your participation becomes. You begin to sense when a market's probability cloud is dense with conflicting expectations and when it's ripe for a decisive collapse. You begin to recognize that your edge is not in knowing, but in positioning yourself where uncertainty is mispriced.

Every decision you make entry, exit, position size is a conscious act of probability collapse. Each represents a statement about what you believe will manifest, balanced by the humility to accept that you could be wrong.

Practical Reflection: Training Conscious Probability Collapsing

To internalize this concept, consider the following reflective exercise:

1. **Map the Probability Cloud:** Before taking a trade, write down every possible scenario you can envision. Assign rough probabilities to each. Notice where your bias leans, and where uncertainty remains high.

2. **Observe the Collapse:** As the trade unfolds, observe which scenario materializes. Was your perceived probability aligned with the outcome? What variables collapsed your expectation news, flow, sentiment, or your own reaction?

3. **Review and Rebuild:** After each trade, update your internal model. Each outcome reshapes your personal probability framework, just as market prices reshape the global one.

This reflective practice turns trading into a conscious experiment in collapsing uncertainty. It transforms each trade into a dialogue with probability, rather than a battle against it.

From Consciousness to Craft

Ultimately, to trade consciously is to understand that markets are not separate from you they are projections of collective consciousness filtered through liquidity, leverage, and emotion. Your observation adds to the whole. Your hesitation, your conviction, your fear they all ripple through the field of market probabilities.

When traders act without awareness, they reinforce noise. When they act with awareness, they refine signal. And when enough aware participants engage consciously, the market itself evolves a self-organizing intelligence that rewards coherence over chaos.

Closing Thought

The market does not simply exist it becomes. Every price is a snapshot of countless collapsed possibilities, a frozen echo of collective intention and fear. In each decision you make, you are both a participant and a creator, collapsing probabilities into the ever-unfolding story of the market.

Trading, then, is not about predicting the next move. It's about cultivating the awareness to see the probability cloud before it collapses and to decide, consciously, how you will participate in that transformation.

Chapter 3

Chaos, Complexity, and Quantum Analogy

Markets do not move in straight lines. They twist, loop, and explode in ways that often defy conventional logic. A small rumor ignites a rally; a single sell order triggers a cascade. What appears chaotic at first glance is, in truth, a complex web of interdependencies dynamic, adaptive, and eerily alive.

This chapter explores the deep structure beneath that apparent chaos. It invites you to look beyond the charts and see markets not as mechanical systems, but as *complex adaptive organisms* ecosystems where feedback loops, emotional contagion, and probabilistic perception converge to shape price.

Chaos theory teaches us that small inputs can produce vast, unpredictable outcomes. **Complexity science** reminds us that markets, like weather systems or neural networks, evolve through nonlinear interactions each trader's decision influencing the next, forming ripples that expand across time and price. And **quantum analogy** offers a poetic but powerful metaphor: that uncertainty, superposition, and entanglement aren't just physics they're woven into the psychology of trading itself.

When you step into the market, you're not entering a static battlefield you're stepping into a dynamic quantum field of possibility, where every observation, every trade, every algorithm adjusts the probabilities for everyone else. Understanding this interplay between chaos and coherence, randomness and structure is key to mastering uncertainty.

In this chapter, we will explore:

- How **nonlinear feedback loops** amplify unpredictability and create emergent behavior in price movement.
- The idea of **interconnected trader ecosystems** how crowds, algorithms, and institutions interact as one collective intelligence.

- And finally, **quantum analogies for price fluctuation**, where uncertainty, observation, and entanglement mirror the very nature of market dynamics.

This isn't just philosophy it's practical awareness. When you grasp chaos not as disorder but as hidden order, you begin to trade differently. You stop searching for control, and start synchronizing with flow. You realize that mastery doesn't mean eliminating uncertainty it means learning to dance with it.

The deeper your awareness of complexity, the clearer your intuition becomes. What once felt random begins to reveal its rhythm. And through that rhythm, the trader evolves from an observer of volatility to a conscious participant in the living, breathing intelligence of the market.

3.1 Nonlinear Feedback Loops and Market Unpredictability

Markets are not machines they are conversations. Every tick, every trade, every algorithmic pulse is part of an ongoing dialogue between human emotion, collective perception, and reactive systems. To understand why markets behave unpredictably, we must first understand the nature of *nonlinearity* how small inputs can trigger disproportionately large effects, how feedback loops amplify emotion, and how chaos emerges not from randomness, but from hidden interconnection.

The Butterfly Effect of Price

In chaos theory, the butterfly effect describes how the flap of a butterfly's wings in Brazil might set off a tornado in Texas. In markets, a similar phenomenon unfolds daily. A hedge fund rebalances its portfolio, slightly adjusting a position. That adjustment changes short-term liquidity, triggering a chain reaction of stop-loss orders and algorithmic trades. Retail traders notice the sudden move, social media amplifies it, and soon, a "trend" is born out of what was once a trivial adjustment.

This is not randomness; it is *sensitivity to initial conditions.* In nonlinear systems like markets, cause and effect are not proportional. The same input on two different days can yield opposite outcomes, depending on the emotional and structural state of participants.

For example, a 0.25% interest rate hike might trigger a panic during a fragile period, yet spark optimism in a bullish environment because it signals confidence. The variable isn't the data point it's the *context* in which the data is perceived. This is the essence of market unpredictability: perception is dynamic, and feedback reshapes it continuously.

The Emotional Amplifier

Every trader, knowingly or not, participates in feedback loops of sentiment. When prices rise, traders feel validated, increasing their conviction and risk appetite. That buying pressure drives prices higher, reinforcing the belief that the market is "strong." Eventually, valuation and logic detach from reality but the loop persists until exhaustion or shock disrupts it.

Similarly, during declines, fear breeds more fear. Selling invites more selling, and algorithms designed to minimize risk amplify volatility. These self-reinforcing spirals are why markets can overshoot both on the upside and downside. They are emotional amplifiers masquerading as rational price discovery mechanisms.

In such loops, information doesn't just reflect fundamentals it reflects *how humans feel about fundamentals*. Prices become the mirror of crowd psychology, oscillating between overconfidence and despair.

Positive vs. Negative Feedback

There are two dominant types of feedback loops that shape market behavior:

- **Positive Feedback:** Reinforces trends. Examples include momentum trading, social validation bias, and algorithmic buying triggered by volatility compression. Positive feedback leads to bubbles, parabolic rises, and euphoric cycles.

- **Negative Feedback:** Restores balance. These are the forces that dampen extremes profit-taking, mean reversion, risk management, and contrarian strategies. Negative feedback brings temporary equilibrium before new cycles emerge.

Markets oscillate between these forces, rarely finding perfect balance. The interplay between positive and negative feedback creates the rhythm of volatility the push and pull between chaos and order.

Complexity Emergence: From Traders to Ecosystems

Imagine the market not as a battlefield of buyers and sellers but as a *living ecosystem*. Each participant retail trader, fund manager, algorithm is an organism reacting to signals, adapting, and competing for survival. The ecosystem evolves as strategies interact, merge, and mutate. What emerges is a self-organizing, adaptive intelligence that no single participant controls, yet everyone influences.

This emergent behavior explains why markets evolve faster than any model can predict. Each feedback loop adds a new layer of complexity. Information no longer flows in a straight line it circulates, refracts, and evolves. Like neurons in a brain, each participant contributes to the collective consciousness of price.

Example: During the 2021 meme stock phenomenon, retail traders coordinated via social media to buy heavily shorted stocks. This created a feedback storm: rising prices forced short-sellers to cover, driving prices even higher. Mainstream media amplified the narrative, drawing in more traders until the loop exhausted itself and reversed violently. This wasn't irrationality; it was a vivid display of nonlinear dynamics in a connected ecosystem.

Why Prediction Fails and Adaptation Wins

Traditional models assume linearity: inputs and outputs maintain proportionate relationships. But markets defy this simplicity. They are *complex adaptive systems* always adjusting, never repeating. In such systems, prediction becomes fragile because each forecast alters the system it seeks to predict.

A trader's job, therefore, is not to predict outcomes but to sense *probabilistic tendencies* to read the flow of interaction, tension, and imbalance. The goal shifts from "being right" to *staying aligned* with how the system evolves in real time.

You cannot forecast chaos, but you can cultivate awareness to move within it.

Practical Reflection: Dancing with Feedback

Exercise 1: Feedback Mapping After a major price move, map the sequence of events backward. Ask: What triggered the initial move? Who reacted next? How did algorithms, media, or sentiment amplify it? Tracing these layers deepens your understanding of how feedback shapes volatility.

Exercise 2: Emotional Echo Awareness During trading, pause and ask yourself: Am I responding to price, or to how others might respond to price? This distinction trains meta-awareness recognizing when you are inside a feedback loop rather than outside observing it.

Exercise 3: Adaptive Mindset Journaling Instead of writing, "I was wrong about the move," reframe it as, "The feedback loop evolved differently than I anticipated." This subtle shift from blame to observation transforms frustration into pattern recognition.

From Control to Conscious Flow

To the conscious trader, unpredictability is not an enemy it is a teacher. The market's nonlinear feedback loops reveal the interconnectedness of all perception and decision. When you see feedback as rhythm rather than randomness, you begin to synchronize with the living pulse of the market. You realize that mastery lies not in control, but in awareness the awareness to adjust, adapt, and evolve with the flow of complexity.

Chaos becomes coherence when met with consciousness. And through that awareness, the trader transcends the illusion of prediction transforming uncertainty into an ally, and feedback into flow.

3.2 Interconnected Trader Ecosystems

The market is often spoken of as if it were a battlefield a place where traders compete, where some win and others lose. But beneath this surface metaphor lies a deeper truth: the market is not a battlefield it is an *ecosystem*. It breathes, adapts, and evolves. Every trader, every algorithm, every decision is a living node in a vast web of interdependence.

This web is the essence of modern market complexity. No participant no matter how powerful acts in isolation. Each trade influences the collective, and the collective, in turn, influences each trader's perception, expectation, and behavior. To understand the market deeply, you must stop thinking as an individual actor and start thinking as a *participant in an emergent intelligence.*

The Ecology of Market Behavior

In nature, ecosystems thrive on balance. Predators depend on prey; plants depend on sunlight and pollinators; rivers carve landscapes but also nourish them. Similarly, financial markets are composed of diverse species retail traders, institutions, high-frequency algorithms, central banks each playing a distinct but interdependent role.

- **Retail traders** provide liquidity and sentiment often the emotional current of the market.
- **Institutional investors** bring long-term capital and structural weight.
- **Algorithms and quant systems** form the nervous system fast, reactive, and data-driven.
- **Market makers** act as stabilizers, ensuring order and price continuity.

When these forces interact, the market becomes more than the sum of its parts it becomes *alive.* The patterns that emerge trends, bubbles, crashes are not random; they are the collective byproduct of countless feedback interactions between these entities.

From Competition to Co-evolution

It is tempting to view trading purely through the lens of competition: one trader's profit is another's loss. But in complex adaptive systems, success comes not from defeating others, but from *co-evolving* with them.

Every trading style exists because others exist. Trend followers thrive because contrarians create reversals. Market makers profit from volatility because directional traders generate it. Each strategy, consciously or not, defines the survival conditions for the rest.

In this sense, traders form a living ecosystem where strategies evolve in response to one another, much like species adapting to environmental pressures. When one becomes dominant say, high-frequency trading others evolve to exploit its weaknesses, restoring balance to the ecosystem. This is why markets resist any single "perfect" model or enduring edge: as soon as an edge is discovered and exploited, the ecosystem adapts, neutralizing it.

Collective Intelligence and Emergence

The emergent behavior of markets arises from countless micro-decisions made under uncertainty. Each trader holds incomplete information, limited perspective, and unique biases. Yet when aggregated, these partial perceptions form a collective intelligence one that reflects a global probability distribution of belief.

The price, then, is not just a number. It is a *consensus signal*, a constantly updating reflection of humanity's collective mind attempting to estimate value under uncertainty.

In this view, markets are not efficient machines but *living consciousness systems* processing information, adapting to new stimuli, and continuously evolving through interaction. This is why attempts to control or predict markets through purely deterministic models often fail: they ignore the *fluid cognition* of the collective.

Example: When Elon Musk tweets about an asset, the information ripple spreads instantly. Algorithms parse sentiment, traders react emotionally, and institutional desks reposition based on expected crowd response. Within seconds, what began as a single expression becomes a global feedback wave. No single actor controls it but everyone contributes to it.

This is emergence: the spontaneous order that arises when millions of independent decisions synchronize briefly around shared perception.

The Conscious Network

To trade consciously within such an interconnected system, you must recognize your dual role as both observer and influencer. Every decision you make whether to buy, sell, or stay still shapes probabilities, however subtly. Awareness of this interplay transforms trading from a reactive game into a participatory art.

Consider the market as a neural network: each trader is a neuron firing with its own bias and input. When collective signals synchronize, trends form just as thoughts emerge in the human mind when neurons fire in coherent patterns. Noise and volatility are not malfunctions; they are part of the system's learning process.

When awareness rises when traders begin to act not from fear or impulse, but from clarity and reflection the network itself evolves. Conscious participation shifts market dynamics from chaos toward coherence, even if only temporarily.

Practical Reflection: Trading Within the Web

Exercise 1: Network Mapping Sketch your perception of the market ecosystem. Identify the players that most influence your trades: retail sentiment, institutions, central banks, or algorithmic flows. Ask: How do my decisions interact with theirs? Where might feedback loops amplify or mute my strategy's impact?

Exercise 2: Mirror Awareness Before entering a trade, ask yourself: "Who am I in this ecosystem right now?" Are you the predator chasing momentum, or the prey reacting to noise? Awareness of your role allows you to adapt more fluidly to changing conditions.

Exercise 3: Collective Pulse Journaling At the end of each trading session, note how collective sentiment felt. Was the market driven by fear, greed, boredom, or anticipation? Over time, this builds intuition for reading *psychological weather patterns* the subtle climate shifts that precede storms or calm.

Interconnection and Responsibility

With awareness of interconnection comes responsibility. When traders act mindlessly chasing trends, amplifying fear, spreading misinformation they contribute to systemic instability. When they act mindfully questioning assumptions, pausing before reacting they dampen unnecessary volatility. The market, in turn, reflects that balance.

A conscious trader understands that every action participates in shaping the collective field. Trading becomes not just about extracting value, but about *harmonizing with flow* finding coherence between personal intent and collective movement.

The Quantum Ecosystem

In quantum systems, particles are entangled the state of one instantly influences another, no matter the distance. In markets, perception operates in a similar way. A trader's belief in London can influence a price move in Tokyo, which reshapes sentiment in New York. Information, emotion, and probability flow through invisible channels of attention and belief.

Understanding this quantum-like interconnection shifts your focus from *reaction* to *resonance*. You begin to trade not from the illusion of isolation but from awareness of interconnected probability fields. Each position you take becomes a note in the market's symphony a contribution to its unfolding pattern.

From Ego to Ecosystem

Most traders begin their journey driven by ego the desire to win, to be right, to outperform. But true mastery comes when ego dissolves into ecosystemic awareness. When you stop fighting the market and start listening to it. When you see your trades not as battles, but as conversations with an evolving intelligence.

In that state, trading becomes meditative. You no longer chase outcomes you respond to flow. You align probability with presence, logic with intuition. And paradoxically, as you relinquish the need for control, your effectiveness increases.

Closing Reflection

The market's complexity is not its curse it is its consciousness. Its unpredictability is not chaos it is creativity. And you, as a trader, are both observer and participant in that creative unfolding.

To master the market is not to dominate it, but to understand your place within its web. When you attune to its rhythms when you feel its pulse through awareness rather than fear you become part of its intelligence. You stop trying to outsmart the ecosystem and begin to *co-evolve* with it.

That is the essence of advanced trading: Not prediction, not control but conscious participation in an ever-adapting, interconnected living system.

3.3 Quantum Analogies for Price Fluctuation

Markets, at their core, resemble quantum systems more than classical machines. Just as quantum particles inhabit states of probability rather than fixed positions, prices in financial markets exist in clouds of potential outcomes until observed, measured, and acted upon. The analogy is not merely poetic it illuminates the hidden structures of uncertainty, perception, and interaction that advanced traders navigate daily.

Price as a Wave of Possibilities

In quantum physics, a particle's location is described by a wave function a mathematical representation of all possible states it could occupy. Only upon measurement does the particle collapse into a definite state.

Similarly, consider a stock or commodity before a major economic announcement. Its price does not simply exist at a single point; it exists in a spectrum of possible levels, each weighted by probability according to market sentiment, liquidity, and expectation. Traders' pre-announcement positions, options pricing, and hedging strategies collectively form a "wave function" of price an ephemeral superposition of potential realities.

Analogy Exercise: Visualize a probability cloud above a stock chart. Each point in the cloud represents a potential price weighted by the likelihood of occurrence. As news hits, trading begins, and orders execute, watch how the cloud collapses, concentrating around a realized price.

Entanglement Across Markets

In quantum mechanics, entangled particles remain connected regardless of distance: an action on one instantly affects the other. Markets exhibit similar phenomena.

When a central bank adjusts interest rates in one country, currency, bond, and equity markets globally respond within seconds. Traders in different time zones, acting on correlated expectations, propagate feedback loops that are instantaneous, complex, and interconnected.

Recognizing this "entanglement" is crucial. Price in one asset class is rarely independent; movements ripple through a web of related markets, creating synchronized probability collapses.

Practical Insight: Map correlations in your portfolio not merely historical ones, but dynamic correlations that shift with sentiment and liquidity. Understand which assets are entangled and anticipate how probability clouds might co-collapse.

Superposition of Outcomes

A key concept in quantum mechanics is superposition: a particle exists in all possible states simultaneously until observed. In trading, the market before resolution behaves similarly.

Consider an option straddle ahead of an earnings report. The stock could soar, plunge, or stagnate. All these outcomes coexist in a probability distribution. Your position is a probe, interacting with this superposition. The act of entering a trade allocating capital does not just respond to one outcome; it becomes part of the system that collapses the range of possibilities.

Reflection Exercise: Before placing a trade, list at least three distinct scenarios for the asset's movement. Assign subjective probabilities to each and consider how your position might influence the realized outcome. This practice sharpens probabilistic intuition and fosters awareness of your participation in the market's emergent reality.

Uncertainty and Observer Effect

In quantum mechanics, the observer influences the observed. In markets, your perception and action also feed back into price dynamics.

A large buy order, for instance, can shift market sentiment before execution completes. Rumors or analyst notes can move prices as if the market "knows" someone is watching. Every participant acts as both observer and influencer, collapsing some range of uncertainty while amplifying others.

Philosophical Insight: Price is not a static truth waiting to be discovered; it is a co-created phenomenon. Your beliefs, attention, and decisions actively shape market reality.

Wave-Particle Duality of Market Behavior

Markets exhibit characteristics analogous to the wave-particle duality:

- **Wave-like behavior:** Trends, momentum, and collective sentiment form oscillations and cycles, observable as waves in charts or probability distributions.
- **Particle-like behavior:** Individual trades, executions, and liquidity events are discrete impacts, manifesting as ticks and price gaps.

Advanced traders recognize that markets oscillate between these modes. Understanding when price behaves like a wave (broad sentiment-driven trends) and when it behaves like a particle (isolated, discrete shocks) is critical for timing, risk management, and strategy selection.

Exercises for Conscious Quantum Trading

1. Probability Visualization Drill: For each trading day, sketch a probability cloud for a target asset. Update it as new information arrives, observing how your subjective probabilities shift. This cultivates awareness of market superposition and your influence on collapse.

2. Entanglement Mapping: Select a portfolio of correlated assets. Track real-time reactions to major news and measure how probability clouds co-move. Identify patterns where entanglement creates early signals of systemic shifts.

3. Observer Awareness Journal: Before executing trades, reflect on your mental state and biases. Document how your actions may influence others' behavior or market perception. Over time, this practice enhances meta-cognition, reducing impulsive decisions and reinforcing conscious participation.

Closing Reflection

Markets are living probability fields, entangled, superposed, and sensitive to observation. The quantum analogy reminds us that trading is not merely prediction it is active engagement with uncertainty.

By embracing the principles of superposition, entanglement, and observer influence, traders cultivate a mindset that balances intuition with analysis, reflection with action. The goal is not to eliminate uncertainty it is to navigate it consciously, recognizing your role in the continuous collapse of possibilities into realized price.

In doing so, you step into a more profound form of market mastery: one that perceives price not just as a number, but as a dynamic reflection of collective perception, probability, and conscious decision-making.

Chapter 4

Entanglement of Markets and Minds

Markets are not merely aggregates of individual trades they are reflections of collective cognition. Every decision, every expectation, and every emotion resonates through the global financial ecosystem, connecting minds across time zones, cultures, and instruments.

This chapter explores the deep entanglement between human psychology and market dynamics. It examines how perceptions, biases, and decisions are not isolated, but interwoven into a network of mutual influence, where the actions of one participant can subtly or dramatically affect the probabilities and outcomes for many others.

4.1 Collective Cognition Across Global Markets

Markets are, at their essence, mirrors of human thought vast, interconnected networks of perception, expectation, and emotion. When we examine them closely, we begin to see that prices are not merely numeric values, but the *aggregate expression of countless minds* attempting to understand, predict, and act within an uncertain world.

The Network of Minds

Imagine for a moment that each trader in the world is a node in a global neural network. Every decision to buy, sell, hedge, or hold is akin to a neuron firing. Individually, each action seems small, almost inconsequential. Yet together, these countless signals form waves of probability that ripple across markets, creating trends, reversals, and emergent phenomena.

Collective cognition emerges from these interactions. It is not a conscious entity, but a phenomenon the way billions of decisions coalesce into a coherent, albeit imperfect, reflection of global perception. Price becomes a real-time snapshot of the collective mind, weighted by sentiment, risk tolerance, and expectation.

Perception as the Driving Force

Each trader interprets information through a personal lens: experience, bias, and context filter every signal. News, economic reports, earnings, geopolitical events none of these are objective triggers; they gain significance only through human interpretation. Collectively, these interpretations aggregate into a probability landscape, where the market moves not according to fundamentals alone, but according to the shared perception of fundamentals.

Example: During the 2008 financial crisis, global markets did not collapse merely because of failing banks. They collapsed because the perception of risk, trust, and future stability spread almost instantaneously across continents. Institutions reacted to perceived reactions of others, creating a cascading effect of fear. The underlying financial instruments were identical before and after the panic; what changed was collective cognition.

Information Waves and Feedback Loops

Markets operate through continuous waves of information. A single event in one part of the world say, a central bank statement in Tokyo travels through the network, filtered by traders, algorithms, and sentiment interpreters. As each participant acts on that information, their decisions generate new signals, feeding back into the system.

This creates feedback loops:

- Positive feedback amplifies trends, driving momentum as more traders act in alignment with perceived direction.
- Negative feedback tempers extremes, as contrarians, regulators, and hedgers act to restore equilibrium.

The combination of these feedbacks shapes the probabilistic contours of price, revealing the dynamics of collective cognition.

Analogies for Understanding Collective Cognition

Consider a flock of birds. Each bird follows simple rules: maintain distance, align with neighbors, and avoid obstacles. Yet without a leader, the flock forms intricate, coordinated patterns. The pattern is not imposed it emerges from local interactions.

Markets function similarly. No central mind dictates every movement; instead, the interactions of many participants create emergent patterns of probability, risk, and opportunity. Recognizing these patterns allows advanced traders to anticipate likely behaviors and align their strategies with emergent flows rather than attempting to dictate outcomes.

Exercises for Engaging with Collective Cognition

Exercise 1: Sentiment Mapping Each day, choose a global market index and identify three major factors influencing trader perception (news, technical signals, macro events). Map how these factors might interact with local and international participants. Ask yourself: How might collective cognition shift if one or more factors change unexpectedly?

Exercise 2: Ripple Observation Select an asset and track price movements after a major global event. Notice how reactions differ across time zones and asset classes. Document when sentiment-driven responses amplify or dampen the initial signal. Reflect on your own position: are you reacting to the event itself, or to the collective perception of the event?

Exercise 3: Probability Cloud Journaling Before entering a trade, sketch a probability cloud reflecting likely outcomes based on observed collective behavior. Include alternative scenarios reflecting divergent interpretations of the same data. As the market unfolds, revisit your cloud and observe how probabilities collapsed, shifted, or persisted.

Reflections on Awareness and Action

Advanced traders recognize that collective cognition is both a constraint and an opportunity. It constrains because no trader acts in isolation; probabilities are shaped by the aggregate. It offers opportunity because awareness of collective sentiment allows for anticipatory positioning, adaptive risk management, and alignment with emergent flows.

Conscious engagement requires three elements:

1. **Observation:** Step back and perceive the market as a reflection of collective thought, not just prices and charts.

2. **Reflection:** Recognize your own biases and how they interact with the broader network.

3. **Action:** Make decisions that align probability, perception, and personal strategy with emergent trends.

Closing Thought

Markets are living mirrors of human cognition. Every trade is a node in a complex network of perception and probability. By cultivating awareness of collective cognition, you gain not only insight but also the ability to act with precision in uncertainty, to navigate the interplay of minds and markets with conscious, probability-informed intention. The conscious trader does not fight the collective mind but listens, interprets, and participates in its unfolding intelligence.

4.2 Interdependence of Trader Behavior

In the complex ecosystem of financial markets, no trader operates in isolation. Every decision whether to buy, sell, hedge, or abstain ripples outward, subtly influencing others. The market is a network of interdependent agents, and understanding this interconnection is essential for advanced trading mastery.

The Web of Influence

Each market participant contributes to a network of expectations. Consider a single institutional investor adjusting a position in a large-cap stock. The trade itself is just one unit, but the market perceives it as a signal. Retail traders may interpret the movement as a trend, algorithms may adjust bids and asks, and even other institutions may recalibrate risk models in response. Within moments, a single action propagates through multiple layers of the market ecosystem, creating emergent behavior far larger than the initiating move.

This interdependence is a form of social computation. Market prices are not only determined by fundamentals but by the perception of other traders' actions. Every order placed contributes to a continuously updating probability distribution of potential outcomes, reflecting collective belief and expectation.

Feedback Loops and Amplification

The interdependence of behavior often manifests as feedback loops:

- **Positive feedback:** When traders collectively perceive an opportunity, their coordinated actions amplify the movement, creating trends or bubbles.
- **Negative feedback:** Conversely, contrarian behaviors, hedging, or profit-taking act as stabilizers, damping extreme movements.

Advanced traders must learn to read these loops. Which behaviors are reinforcing each other? Which are counteracting? Recognizing the source and direction of feedback allows for more precise risk management and strategic alignment.

Analogy: Imagine a school of fish navigating a predator-laden reef. Each fish adjusts based on the movement of its neighbors. Some motions amplify a collective escape response, while others create localized eddies of indecision. Similarly, in markets, the interdependence of traders' behaviors creates waves, surges, and eddies of price action.

Cognitive Coupling and Shared Biases

Interdependence extends beyond observable trades to cognition itself. Traders often share mental models, biases, and heuristics. When many participants overvalue momentum, underweight risk, or react emotionally to headlines, collective behavior becomes predictable in patterns albeit probabilistically rather than deterministically.

Understanding this shared cognition is key to anticipating market reactions. If the majority interprets an economic report one way, the market response is amplified not because the data changed intrinsically, but because perceptions are coupled. Awareness of these cognitive linkages allows the conscious trader to position with a probabilistic advantage.

Practical Exercises for Engaging with Interdependence

Exercise 1: Trade Ripple Mapping Select a trade idea and map its potential influence across participants: retail traders, institutional desks, algorithmic strategies. Visualize how the decision may create ripples through price, sentiment, and liquidity.

Exercise 2: Feedback Loop Identification During market hours, track price movements in response to a series of trades or news events. Identify patterns of amplification (positive feedback) and damping (negative feedback). Ask: How could your position interact with these loops?

Exercise 3: Bias Awareness Journaling Document your expectations before entering a trade. Then note how other market participants might share or contradict these beliefs. Over time, this builds insight into coupled behavior and enhances probabilistic thinking.

Ethical and Strategic Considerations

Interdependence implies responsibility. Every trade contributes to market dynamics, sometimes stabilizing, sometimes destabilizing. Advanced traders recognize that conscious, deliberate action can align with systemic stability rather than unintentionally amplifying risk.

Strategically, understanding interdependence enables:

- Anticipation of cascading effects from large trades.
- Timing entries and exits to leverage collective behavior rather than compete against it.
- Designing adaptive strategies that adjust as the network of trader behavior evolves.

Reflection on Conscious Participation

To trade effectively within interdependent systems, one must cultivate both awareness and humility. Awareness of your impact allows for precise alignment with market flows. Humility reminds you that the system is larger than any single participant; outcomes are probabilistic, not guaranteed.

Guiding Principle: Think of your trading decisions as interactions in a living organism. Each action contributes to the organism's health and behavior, even if subtly. By acting with conscious intention and probabilistic awareness, you align yourself with the adaptive intelligence of the market, rather than merely reacting to it.

Closing Thought

Interdependence transforms markets from arenas of isolated competition into ecosystems of collective cognition. Mastery arises not from attempting to control others' behavior, but from understanding it mapping, anticipating, and harmonizing with the web of interactions that drive price. The conscious trader thrives within this web, leveraging insight, reflection, and probabilistic decision-making to navigate complexity with clarity and purpose.

4.3 Emotional and Cognitive Entanglement

In financial markets, entanglement is not solely the domain of price or liquidity; it extends deeply into the human mind. Emotions, perceptions, and cognitive frameworks are intertwined, creating networks of influence that ripple through markets in subtle yet profound ways. Understanding this emotional and cognitive entanglement is essential for advanced traders seeking conscious, probability-aligned decision-making.

The Interwoven Mind of the Market

Every trader brings a unique cognitive lens to the market shaped by experience, education, temperament, and biases. Yet these lenses are not isolated. They influence and are influenced by the decisions of others, creating a shared, emergent psychology that drives market behavior.

Consider a sudden, unexpected geopolitical event. Some traders may react with fear, others with opportunistic excitement. The interplay of these emotions fear amplifying selling pressure, hope catalyzing buying generates complex patterns in price movements. This is emotional entanglement: a network of feelings interacting to shape probabilistic outcomes in real-time.

Cognitive Coupling and Market Dynamics

Cognition in trading is equally entangled. Traders interpret information through mental models, heuristics, and frameworks, many of which are shared across institutions or communities. When large groups rely on similar models such as moving averages, sentiment indicators, or risk metrics their decisions become correlated, even if unconsciously.

This cognitive coupling can create predictable yet probabilistic market behaviors:

- **Herding behavior:** Multiple participants converge on similar interpretations, amplifying trends.
- **Contrarian opportunities:** Recognizing where shared cognitive biases may overinflate probabilities enables strategic positioning.
- **Volatility surges:** When entrenched models fail, simultaneous adjustments create rapid, unpredictable fluctuations.

Analogies for Emotional-Cognitive Entanglement

Imagine a symphony orchestra. Each musician interprets the conductor's cues and the surrounding ensemble, blending individual expression with collective harmony. A single musician reacting too early or too late can alter the performance, creating ripples that affect the entire soundscape. Markets operate similarly: each trader's mind is an instrument, tuned by emotion and cognition, collectively producing the probabilistic "music" of price.

Exercises for Conscious Awareness

Exercise 1: Emotional Mapping Before trading, identify your current emotional state fearful, excited, anxious, calm and note potential biases it may introduce. Observe how these emotions interact with perceived market sentiment. Over time, track patterns: Which emotions amplify risk? Which facilitate clarity?

Exercise 2: Cognitive Checkpoints Select a trade idea and outline the mental models informing your decision (e.g., trend analysis, valuation frameworks, risk heuristics). Consider how other market participants may be using similar or conflicting models. Reflect: Could collective reliance on these models create predictable collapses or expansions in probability distributions?

Exercise 3: Entanglement Journaling Maintain a daily log of observed market behaviors alongside your own reactions. Note instances where your emotional or cognitive state appeared to align with or diverge from the broader market. Analyze how this alignment or misalignment impacted trade outcomes, refining awareness of entanglement patterns.

Practical Insights for Traders

1. **Anticipate Emotional Contagion:** Large moves often reflect not only fundamentals but waves of collective emotion. Awareness allows you to position strategically, harnessing momentum or hedging against irrational exuberance or panic.

2. **Leverage Cognitive Diversity:** Avoid relying solely on one framework. Integrate multiple models to reduce vulnerability to shared biases and enhance probabilistic reasoning.

3. **Align Action with Awareness:** Recognize that your decisions influence the collective mind, just as it influences you. Mindful trading transforms entanglement from a source of risk into a tool for adaptive, conscious participation.

Reflective Philosophy

Emotional and cognitive entanglement reminds us that trading is fundamentally human. Markets are reflections not only of capital but of perception, judgment, and feeling. Attempting to isolate oneself from this web is futile; conscious traders instead observe, understand, and navigate it with awareness.

The goal is not emotional detachment but emotional intelligence a deliberate engagement with entangled minds, including your own. By cultivating awareness of how thoughts, beliefs, and feelings propagate through markets, you transform entanglement from a source of uncertainty into a compass for probabilistic, mindful action.

Closing Thought

Advanced market mastery emerges when traders recognize that price movements are inseparable from the collective mind and its emotional-cognitive entanglements. The conscious trader cultivates clarity amidst complexity, perception amidst uncertainty, and alignment amidst interdependence. In doing so, one navigates the market not as a passive observer, but as an aware participant shaping and being shaped by the intricate web of minds that defines financial reality.

Chapter 5

Observing the Unobservable

Markets are shaped by forces that are often hidden from plain view. Prices, volumes, and indicators reveal only part of the story; beneath the surface lie subtle dynamics psychological, probabilistic, and systemic that govern market behavior.

This chapter delves into the realm of the unobservable: the hidden variables, cognitive blind spots, and perceptual biases that influence trading outcomes. We explore how advanced traders can cultivate heightened awareness, detect patterns invisible to conventional analysis, and align observation with deliberate, conscious action.

Here, the focus shifts from what is easily seen to what is felt, intuited, or inferred the underlying currents that move markets beyond charts and models. Through reflection, exercises, and practical frameworks, readers will learn to perceive the unseen, reduce the impact of biases, and make decisions that resonate with both probabilistic reality and mindful insight.

5.1 Hidden Variables and Behavioral Blind Spots

In financial markets, the visible metrics price charts, volume, and indicators are only the tip of the iceberg. Beneath this observable layer lie hidden variables: factors that influence outcomes but remain unmeasured, misunderstood, or entirely invisible. Simultaneously, traders themselves are subject to behavioral blind spots cognitive distortions and biases that obscure awareness and skew perception. Mastery requires both the identification of these hidden forces and the disciplined cultivation of awareness to mitigate their influence.

The Nature of Hidden Variables

Hidden variables are the unseen currents shaping market probabilities. They include macroeconomic interdependencies, latent risk factors, algorithmic feedback loops, and collective sentiment shifts that rarely appear in conventional data feeds.

Consider, for example, liquidity risk in an asset that appears stable. A sudden withdrawal of counterparties a hidden variable can trigger cascading price adjustments. Similarly, the collective positioning of leveraged players may remain invisible until a small perturbation uncovers a wave of forced reactions. Recognizing that such variables exist, even when they cannot be quantified precisely, allows the advanced trader to approach markets probabilistically rather than deterministically.

Behavioral Blind Spots

Human cognition is imperfect. We rely on heuristics mental shortcuts to make sense of complex information, but these shortcuts create blind spots. Common examples include:

- **Confirmation bias:** Seeing only the data that supports preexisting beliefs.
- **Recency bias:** Overweighting the influence of recent events on future expectations.
- **Overconfidence:** Overestimating the accuracy of one's own predictions or models.

These blind spots are not flaws to be eliminated they are features of human cognition. The challenge is to observe them, understand their influence, and design decision-making processes that account for their probabilistic impact.

Analogies for Awareness

Imagine navigating a dense fog while steering a ship. The visible horizon provides some guidance, but much of the terrain is obscured. Relying solely on sight leads to collisions with unseen obstacles. Sensors, instruments, and prior knowledge help anticipate the hidden currents beneath the surface. Similarly, in markets, observation alone is insufficient; traders must cultivate frameworks to perceive the unobservable currents influencing price action.

Practical Exercises

Exercise 1: Blind Spot Journaling Before each trading session, list potential cognitive biases that may influence your decisions. Throughout the day, track decisions and outcomes, noting when these biases emerged and how they affected your judgments. Over time, patterns reveal habitual blind spots and provide targets for conscious adjustment.

Exercise 2: Hidden Variable Mapping Choose a market or asset and brainstorm factors not reflected in conventional data feeds that could influence its price. Include macroeconomic, psychological, and systemic elements. Assign a subjective probability to each factor affecting potential outcomes, and incorporate these probabilities into your trade planning.

Exercise 3: Scenario Visualization Imagine the market behaving contrary to your expectations due to an unseen variable or collective bias. Map how different participant types retail, institutional, algorithmic might respond. Use this exercise to rehearse adaptive strategies and expand your probabilistic thinking.

Reflection on Observation

Advanced trading is as much about what is unseen as what is seen. Hidden variables and behavioral blind spots are constant companions in the probabilistic landscape of the market. The conscious trader cultivates an awareness that is both humble and vigilant, acknowledging uncertainty while actively seeking to understand it.

This mindset transforms uncertainty from a source of fear into a navigable space for probabilistic reasoning. By observing the unobservable, traders align perception, probability, and action, enabling decisions that are informed, flexible, and deeply conscious.

Closing Thought

The true frontier of market mastery lies beyond charts and indicators. It resides in the ability to perceive hidden currents, recognize cognitive distortions, and act with intentionality within uncertainty. Embracing this challenge elevates trading from reactive speculation to conscious engagement, where insight, reflection, and probabilistic awareness guide action in a world defined by complexity and interconnection.

5.2 Biases in Market Perception

Markets are not merely aggregations of numbers and data points they are mirrors of human perception, interpretation, and expectation. Yet, perception is rarely neutral. It is filtered through cognitive lenses, shaped by emotion, experience, and habitual thinking patterns. These filters, while necessary for navigating complexity, introduce biases that subtly distort how traders interpret information, assess probability, and make decisions.

Understanding Perceptual Biases

Perceptual biases are systematic deviations in the way information is processed. They influence the perceived significance of events, the weighting of evidence, and even the interpretation of risk. Common examples include:

- **Anchoring:** Over-reliance on initial information or reference points, such as a prior high or low price, which skews probability assessment.
- **Availability heuristic:** Estimating likelihood based on the ease with which examples come to mind, often exaggerating recent or dramatic events.
- **Hindsight bias:** Viewing past market movements as more predictable than they actually were, leading to overconfidence in forecasting.
- **Loss aversion:** Assigning disproportionate weight to potential losses relative to gains, shaping risk-taking behavior.

These biases are not mere inconveniences they are active forces shaping market dynamics. When large groups of traders share similar biases, collective distortions emerge, creating trends, volatility spikes, and anomalies that may appear "irrational" from a purely fundamental standpoint.

Analogies for Insight

Consider a prism through which light passes. The spectrum observed depends on the prism's shape and material; light itself does not change. Similarly, the market presents objective information, but perception acts as a cognitive prism. Two traders can observe the same chart, the same news, and the same economic data, yet interpret the signals differently due to perceptual filters. Awareness of the prism enables traders to consciously adjust their interpretation and expand their probabilistic horizon.

Practical Exercises for Advanced Traders

Exercise 1: Bias Identification and Logging Maintain a bias journal for each trading session. Before entering a trade, identify which perceptual biases may influence your interpretation of market data. After the trade, evaluate how those biases manifested and affected decision outcomes. Over time, this practice sharpens meta-cognition and heightens awareness of recurring distortions.

Exercise 2: Counterfactual Analysis Select a recent market move and reconstruct it from multiple perspectives. Ask: How would traders with different biases perceive this event? Visualize scenarios where overconfidence, loss aversion, or anchoring could produce divergent actions. This expands probabilistic thinking and prepares you for unexpected market reactions.

Exercise 3: Perspective Shifting Before executing a trade, consciously challenge your first impression. Ask yourself: What am I missing? Which signals might I be overvaluing? Document alternative interpretations and assign subjective probabilities to each. This mental flexibility reduces the risk of being trapped by perceptual bias.

Cognitive Awareness and Probabilistic Alignment

Recognizing biases is not enough; advanced traders must integrate this awareness into a framework of probabilistic decision-making. Each market observation should be processed with an understanding that perception is inherently filtered. By adjusting for biases, traders enhance the fidelity of their probability estimates, enabling decisions that are more aligned with reality rather than their subjective lens.

Reflective Insights

Biases are an intrinsic part of human cognition, but they need not dictate outcomes. The conscious trader treats perception as a variable, not a given, and employs reflection, journaling, and scenario exercises to reveal distortions. By consciously managing perceptual biases, traders align their mental models more closely with probabilistic market reality, cultivating clarity amidst uncertainty.

Closing Thought

Market mastery is as much about the mind as it is about strategy. Biases in perception are invisible currents that shape waves of collective behavior. By observing, reflecting, and adjusting for these biases, the trader transforms unseen distortions into actionable insight, bridging awareness and probability into decisions that are conscious, adaptive, and aligned with the fluid intelligence of the market.

5.3 Aligning Observation, Awareness, and Action

Observation alone is insufficient in the complex, probabilistic ecosystem of financial markets. To navigate uncertainty effectively, traders must integrate three interdependent faculties: observing the market, cultivating conscious awareness of their own cognitive and emotional processes, and translating these insights into deliberate action. This triad observation, awareness, and action forms the foundation of conscious trading.

From Observation to Understanding

Observation is the first step, but it is more than passively watching price charts or monitoring indicators. It is the disciplined practice of perceiving patterns, anomalies, and signals without immediate judgment. Observation involves:

- **Capturing data with precision:** Recording market variables, price movements, volume flows, and sentiment indicators accurately.
- **Noticing anomalies:** Detecting divergences, unexpected correlations, or subtle shifts in market behavior.
- **Contextualizing information:** Placing observations within broader temporal, systemic, and probabilistic frameworks.

Analogy: Imagine a musician listening to an orchestra. They do not merely hear individual notes; they perceive harmonics, timing, and interaction. Similarly, the conscious trader observes not only individual price movements but the interplay of orders, sentiment, and emergent patterns.

Cultivating Awareness

Awareness is the internal counterpart to external observation. It is the reflective space where traders recognize their own biases, emotional states, and cognitive models. Awareness allows traders to separate perception from reaction, observation from judgment, and data from interpretation.

Practical Exercise 1: Awareness Checkpoints Before entering the market, pause for a brief mental scan:

- What emotions am I experiencing fear, greed, anticipation?
- Which cognitive biases might color my interpretation of the data?
- Am I perceiving patterns objectively or imposing preconceptions?

By systematically checking in, traders enhance the fidelity of their perception and reduce the probability of impulsive, bias-driven actions.

Action: Translating Insight into Decisions

Action is the culmination of observation and awareness. It is not reactive; it is probabilistic, deliberate, and adaptive. A conscious trader acts in alignment with the signals observed, filtered through self-awareness and tempered by a probabilistic understanding of uncertainty.

Practical Exercise 2: Probabilistic Decision Framework For any potential trade:

1. List observed signals and data points.

2. Assess probabilities for multiple scenarios, considering hidden variables and market interdependence.

3. Align intended action with both probabilistic assessment and emotional state, ensuring decisions are deliberate rather than reactive.

4. Execute action with mindful attention, and immediately record rationale and expectations.

This exercise reinforces a feedback loop, allowing observation and awareness to continually inform future actions.

Integrating Observation, Awareness, and Action

Alignment requires practice, reflection, and iterative refinement. The advanced trader cultivates a continuous loop:

1. Observe: Gather data, notice subtle signals, and contextualize information.

2. Reflect: Assess biases, emotional states, and cognitive models influencing perception.

3. Decide and Act: Translate insight into probabilistic, deliberate action, while remaining open to adaptation.

Exercise 3: Daily Alignment Journal End each trading day with a structured reflection:

- What did I observe that I did not initially anticipate?
- How did my emotional or cognitive state influence my interpretation?
- Did my actions align with my observations and awareness?
- What adjustments can I make tomorrow to improve alignment?

This ritual strengthens the trader's ability to harmonize mind and market, perception and probability.

Philosophical Perspective

Markets are probabilistic mirrors of human behavior, yet they also respond to conscious engagement. Observation without awareness is shallow; awareness without action is inert; action without reflection is reckless. True mastery arises when these elements are consciously integrated, creating a dynamic equilibrium between perception, cognition, and behavior.

Closing Thought

Aligning observation, awareness, and action transforms trading from a reactive struggle into an adaptive, reflective practice. It empowers traders to navigate complexity with clarity, to act in harmony with emergent probabilities, and to engage with markets not as chaotic adversaries but as living systems whose underlying patterns can be intuited, observed, and consciously influenced. In this alignment, uncertainty becomes an opportunity for insight, and each decision becomes a deliberate step toward mastery.

Part II

The Trader's Conscious Mind

Chapter 6

Conscious vs Subconscious Decision-Making

Trading is as much a journey within the mind as it is an interaction with markets. Every decision arises from the interplay between conscious reasoning and subconscious processing. While conscious thought allows deliberate analysis and structured strategy, the subconscious continuously processes vast amounts of information, detecting patterns, signaling risks, and guiding intuitive judgments.

This chapter explores the dynamic relationship between these two modes of cognition. We will examine how intuition functions as a sophisticated data processor, how cognitive biases distort probability assessments, and how advanced traders can cultivate awareness to sharpen clarity and focus. By understanding and harmonizing conscious and subconscious decision-making, traders can transform instinctual reactions into informed, probabilistic, and mindful actions.

6.1 Intuition as a Data Processor

Intuition is often misunderstood as a mysterious, almost mystical sense that guides decisions without reason. For advanced traders, however, intuition is far from irrational it is the mind's high-speed, subconscious data processor. It integrates vast amounts of sensory input, market experience, emotional cues, and probabilistic inference, synthesizing patterns that may elude conscious analysis. Understanding intuition as a sophisticated computational system transforms it from a vague "gut feeling" into a tool of conscious trading mastery.

The Subconscious Market Scanner

Consider the subconscious mind as a parallel processing engine. While the conscious mind focuses on specific charts, news, or metrics, the subconscious continuously scans an enormous landscape of cues: micro-price movements, correlations, liquidity shifts, sentiment flows, and past experiences. It recognizes anomalies, predicts trends, and often signals potential outcomes before the conscious mind has fully processed the information.

Analogy: Imagine a pilot navigating turbulent skies. Instruments provide explicit data, but years of experience allow the pilot to feel subtle shifts in wind, turbulence, and engine vibration. This tacit awareness guides micro-adjustments that maintain stability and optimize performance. Similarly, a trader's intuition senses patterns and probabilities in the market, enabling timely and adaptive responses.

Intuition as Probabilistic Integration

Intuition excels in probabilistic reasoning because it aggregates fragments of information into coherent mental models. It does not generate deterministic predictions; instead, it signals likelihoods, risk concentrations, and emergent trends. For example, a trader may "feel" a breakout is imminent not from conscious calculation of support and resistance alone, but from an integrated assessment of price action, volume anomalies, and market sentiment accumulated over time.

Exercises for Enhancing Intuitive Processing

Exercise 1: Pattern Immersion Spend time observing market behavior without executing trades. Track price movements, order flow, and volatility patterns. Over time, the subconscious absorbs these patterns, strengthening intuitive recognition of probabilistic signals.

Exercise 2: Intuition Journaling Before executing a trade, note your initial intuitive assessment of potential outcomes. Compare with the actual unfolding of the market afterward. Record discrepancies, patterns of alignment, and cues that triggered correct or incorrect intuitions. This reflective practice refines the subconscious processing engine.

Exercise 3: Sensory Awareness Drills Develop acute attention to subtle market cues: minute changes in volume, bid-ask spread, or correlations across assets. Pair observation with reflective pauses, allowing the subconscious to integrate patterns into actionable intuition.

Balancing Intuition with Conscious Reasoning

Intuition alone is insufficient; unchecked, it may succumb to biases, overconfidence, or emotional distortion. The conscious mind provides structure, discipline, and probabilistic validation. The synergy emerges when traders treat intuition as a data processor:

- **Observe intuitions without judgment:** Record what your subconscious signals.
- **Analyze consciously:** Evaluate intuitive insights against probabilistic reasoning and empirical data.
- **Act mindfully:** Combine intuitive insight with deliberate, probability-informed action.

Reflective Insights

Intuition is the bridge between perception and probability, subconscious insight and conscious action. Advanced traders cultivate this faculty not by ignoring logic, but by training the mind to recognize patterns, integrate experience, and signal probabilistic tendencies. The conscious trader learns to trust intuition as a probabilistic guide, while continuously verifying, adjusting, and aligning it with reasoned judgment.

Closing Thought

Markets communicate in whispers, subtle shifts, and emergent patterns. Intuition allows the trader to hear what the conscious mind may initially miss. By understanding intuition as a data processor, observing its signals, and integrating them with deliberate reasoning, traders transform ephemeral "gut feelings" into actionable, probability-aligned decisions navigating complexity with clarity, adaptability, and conscious insight.

6.2 Cognitive Biases as Probability Distorters

In the intricate landscape of trading, our minds serve as both instruments and obstacles. While they enable rapid pattern recognition and probabilistic inference, they are also susceptible to cognitive biases that subtly distort perception, misalign probability estimates, and influence decisions. For the advanced trader, understanding biases is not merely academic it is essential for transforming intuition and observation into accurate, probability-aligned action.

The Mechanics of Bias

Cognitive biases are systematic errors in judgment that arise from the mind's attempt to simplify complexity. They are heuristics mental shortcuts that allow fast decision-making but at the cost of probabilistic fidelity. Biases distort the perception of likelihood, inflate confidence, and skew risk-reward assessments.

Common biases affecting trading include:

- **Confirmation Bias:** Favoring information that validates pre-existing beliefs, often ignoring contradictory evidence.
- **Recency Bias:** Overweighting recent events when estimating probabilities of future outcomes.
- **Overconfidence Bias:** Overestimating the accuracy of one's own predictions, leading to excessive risk-taking.
- **Availability Bias:** Judging probability based on how easily examples come to mind, rather than statistical reality.
- **Loss Aversion:** Assigning greater weight to potential losses than equivalent gains, affecting position sizing and exit strategies.

Each bias acts like a lens, refracting probabilities away from objective reality and subtly reshaping the trader's mental map of the market.

Analogy: The Probabilistic Prism

Imagine viewing the market through a prism that distorts light in specific directions. Even when the underlying data is unchanged, the lens of bias refracts perception, producing patterns that seem familiar but may be misleading. A trader anchored to a previous high may overestimate the probability of a breakout, while one swayed by recent volatility may overreact to minor fluctuations. Awareness of these distortions allows the trader to recalibrate, adjusting probabilistic judgments to more accurately reflect market realities.

Exercises for Advanced Traders

Exercise 1: Bias Identification and Probability Calibration For each trading decision, explicitly identify potential biases. Ask: "Which heuristics might distort my perception of probability?" Adjust your probability estimates accordingly and document the rationale. Over time, this practice builds meta-cognitive awareness and improves probabilistic accuracy.

Exercise 2: Contrarian Scenario Analysis Select a current trade idea and construct a scenario where the market moves against your expectation. Identify which biases might lead you to underestimate this risk. Assess the probability of this counter-scenario, and design hedges or contingency plans to manage potential outcomes.

Exercise 3: Retrospective Bias Mapping Review past trades and classify errors according to cognitive bias. Did overconfidence lead to excessive risk? Did recency bias obscure long-term trends? This retrospective mapping converts experience into structured learning and probabilistic refinement.

Integrating Awareness into Decision-Making

Recognizing biases is only the first step; integration into a probabilistic framework is essential. Advanced traders build a feedback loop:

1. Observe market signals and intuitive insights.
2. Identify potential cognitive distortions affecting probability assessment.
3. Adjust estimates and strategies to account for these distortions.
4. Act with deliberate, conscious attention to alignment between perception and reality.

This loop transforms bias from an unseen saboteur into a navigable element of market cognition.

Reflective Insight

Cognitive biases are neither inherently negative nor avoidable; they are integral features of human cognition. The conscious trader treats them as variables to be measured, understood, and managed. By aligning observation, intuition, and probabilistic reasoning, biases become not obstacles but data points in a meta-cognitive feedback system, enhancing decision quality rather than diminishing it.

Closing Thought

Markets are probabilistic systems, yet human cognition is imperfect. Biases distort the lens through which probabilities are perceived, influencing every decision. Advanced traders develop the skill of recognizing, mapping, and compensating for these distortions, converting cognitive vulnerabilities into structured insight. In doing so, the probabilistic mind achieves clarity, integrating awareness, intuition, and conscious action to navigate uncertainty with precision and philosophical depth.

6.3 Training Awareness for Clarity and Focus

Awareness is the cornerstone of conscious trading. It is the lens through which observation, intuition, and probabilistic reasoning converge into deliberate action. Without sustained awareness, even the most sophisticated models, the sharpest intuition, and the most disciplined strategies can be distorted by emotional noise, cognitive bias, or fleeting distractions. Training awareness is not merely a mental exercise it is a systematic cultivation of clarity, focus, and presence, transforming the mind into a reliable instrument for navigating the probabilistic currents of the market.

The Nature of Awareness in Trading

Awareness is both a state and a skill. As a state, it is the conscious observation of the present moment, uncolored by habitual judgment or reactive emotion. As a skill, it is the practiced ability to maintain this state under conditions of uncertainty, volatility, and psychological pressure.

Consider awareness as the trading equivalent of a telescope: a finely tuned instrument that allows the trader to perceive distant patterns, subtle anomalies, and probabilistic signals that remain invisible to an untrained mind.

Exercises for Enhancing Clarity and Focus

Exercise 1: Mindful Observation of Market Micro-Movements Select a specific market or asset and observe it without judgment for a set period (e.g., 30 minutes). Note patterns, subtle correlations, and divergences without attempting to act. The objective is to separate pure observation from the impulse to react, allowing the subconscious to process information before the conscious mind intervenes.

Exercise 2: Attention Partitioning Drill Divide market variables into categories: technical indicators, macroeconomic news, sentiment signals, and liquidity flows. Practice shifting awareness deliberately among categories, observing each with focused attention for short intervals. This trains cognitive flexibility, reduces tunnel vision, and enhances the ability to integrate multiple probabilistic streams simultaneously.

Exercise 3: Awareness Journaling After each trading session, record not only actions and outcomes but also states of awareness:

- When did I feel fully present, and when did my focus drift?
- What emotional states influenced my perception and decision-making?
- Which distractions or biases subtly affected my probabilistic judgment?

This reflective practice strengthens meta-awareness and provides a structured map of attention over time.

Integrating Awareness into Decision-Making

Clarity and focus are not ends in themselves; they are functional tools that enhance the reliability of probabilistic assessment and intuitive insight. The conscious trader integrates awareness into the decision-making cycle as follows:

1. **Observe:** Collect market data and intuitive impressions without immediate judgment.
2. **Reflect:** Examine personal cognitive and emotional states that may distort perception.

3. **Probabilize:** Assess probabilities using both data-driven models and intuitive insights filtered through heightened awareness.

4. **Act:** Execute decisions aligned with conscious attention, integrating clarity, focus, and probabilistic reasoning.

This alignment creates a feedback loop: awareness enhances perception, perception informs probability, and probability guides conscious action, reinforcing a cycle of continuous refinement.

Philosophical Perspective

Awareness in trading is akin to tuning an instrument before a performance. An untuned instrument produces noise, no matter how skilled the musician. Similarly, an inattentive mind introduces distortions into every observation, intuition, and probabilistic judgment. By cultivating awareness, traders attune their internal instrument, harmonizing perception, cognition, and action, and enabling a fluid, responsive engagement with the market's inherent uncertainty.

Closing Thought

Clarity and focus are not static achievements but ongoing practices, cultivated through deliberate exercises, reflective journaling, and mindful engagement with market dynamics. For the advanced trader, awareness is both shield and compass: it filters cognitive distortions, clarifies probabilistic signals, and directs conscious action. In mastering awareness, traders transform the mind into a precision tool, capable of navigating complexity with insight, calm, and adaptive intelligence. Ultimately, the cultivation of awareness is the foundation upon which all conscious, probability-informed trading is built.

Chapter 7

Mental Superposition

In financial markets, uncertainty is not an obstacle to be eliminated but a reality to be embraced. Advanced traders recognize that any given market situation can evolve into multiple, simultaneously plausible outcomes. Mental superposition is the ability to hold these possibilities in mind without prematurely collapsing them into a single prediction, enabling probabilistic reasoning, adaptive decision-making, and emotional resilience.

This chapter explores the concept of mental superposition, its relevance for trading under uncertainty, and practical strategies for expanding cognitive flexibility. We will examine how to hold multiple outcomes simultaneously, make decisions without collapsing possibilities prematurely, and engage in exercises designed to strengthen the mind's capacity to navigate complex, probabilistic environments.

7.1 Holding Multiple Outcomes Simultaneously

The mind of a seasoned trader is not a single-lane highway; it is a multidimensional landscape capable of holding competing possibilities without collapsing into premature certainty. Holding multiple outcomes simultaneously what we term *mental superposition* is an essential skill for navigating the probabilistic nature of financial markets. It allows traders to perceive the market as a spectrum of probabilities rather than a sequence of deterministic events, transforming uncertainty from a source of fear into a tool for strategic insight.

The Philosophy of Superposition

In classical thinking, decision-making is often framed as selecting the "correct" path among many. Yet markets are rarely deterministic. Each tick, trade, and announcement creates a web of possible trajectories. Mental superposition encourages the trader to hold these possibilities in mind, acknowledging that multiple futures coexist until the market evolves and "collapses" one trajectory into observable reality.

Analogy: Consider a chess grandmaster analyzing a complex position. They do not commit to a single line immediately; instead, they hold several plausible variations simultaneously, mentally evaluating responses, risks, and contingencies before choosing a move. Similarly, the advanced trader maintains a probabilistic map of potential market outcomes, enabling more flexible, adaptive responses.

Cognitive Mechanics

Holding multiple outcomes simultaneously engages both the conscious and subconscious mind:

- **Conscious Layer:** Deliberate comparison of scenarios, weighing probabilities, and aligning actions with risk tolerance.
- **Subconscious Layer:** Intuitive sensing of pattern shifts, correlations, and emergent signals that may alter probabilities in real-time.

The interplay between these layers allows for dynamic adjustments: the conscious mind evaluates, while the subconscious monitors subtle cues, together enabling probabilistic agility.

Practical Exercises

Exercise 1: Scenario Mapping For a given trading opportunity, map at least three distinct potential outcomes. Assign a subjective probability to each, considering technical, fundamental, and sentiment factors. Periodically update these probabilities as new information emerges, noting how your intuition and observation influence adjustments.

Exercise 2: Probability Journaling Before executing a trade, write down all plausible scenarios, including unlikely but possible extremes. After market movements unfold, compare your mental superposition with reality. Reflect on where probabilities were under- or overestimated and identify patterns in your intuitive judgment.

Exercise 3: Superposition Visualization Visualize multiple price paths on a mental or physical chart simultaneously. Imagine the market "splitting" into parallel trajectories, each with its own probability cloud. This strengthens the ability to maintain cognitive flexibility without prematurely committing to a single outcome.

Integrating Superposition into Trading Decisions

Mental superposition is not indecision; it is a disciplined method for managing uncertainty:

1. **Observe:** Gather market signals and identify relevant variables.
2. **Enumerate:** List multiple plausible outcomes with estimated probabilities.
3. **Align:** Ensure your emotional state and risk tolerance are compatible with the range of scenarios.
4. **Act:** Execute trades based on probabilistic weighting rather than a single deterministic forecast.
5. **Reflect:** Post-trade analysis to refine future mental superposition and probability assessment.

Philosophical Reflection

Embracing mental superposition cultivates humility, patience, and cognitive resilience. It recognizes the limits of foresight, allowing traders to coexist with uncertainty rather than struggle against it. By holding multiple outcomes in mind, traders enhance their ability to adapt, innovate, and respond dynamically to the ever-shifting landscape of markets.

Closing Thought

Markets are inherently probabilistic, and certainty is an illusion. The advanced trader learns to inhabit the space between possibilities, to perceive the market as a spectrum of potentialities, and to act with both decisiveness and cognitive flexibility. Mental superposition transforms uncertainty from a source of anxiety into a platform for probabilistic insight, enabling decisions that are both informed and adaptive, grounded in observation, probability, and conscious awareness.

7.2 Making Decisions Amid Uncertainty

Uncertainty is the essence of financial markets. No model, no chart, no algorithm can fully capture the infinite variables that drive price movement. For advanced traders, uncertainty is not a threat it is the raw material from which opportunity emerges. Making decisions amid uncertainty requires a profound alignment of perception, probability, and conscious awareness, transforming the market's inherent ambiguity into actionable insight.

The Nature of Uncertainty

Markets are probabilistic systems. Every price level, trend, or breakout represents a spectrum of potential outcomes influenced by countless factors: macroeconomic shifts, geopolitical events, investor sentiment, algorithmic trading behavior, and even collective human psychology. Decision-making under uncertainty demands that we accept the limits of foresight while cultivating the ability to act effectively within those limits.

Analogy: Consider a sailor navigating foggy waters. The horizon is obscured, currents shift unpredictably, and unseen obstacles lurk beneath the surface. Yet the sailor does not remain motionless. Instead, they use experience, instrumentation, and constant observation to make probabilistic decisions, adjusting sails and course iteratively. Similarly, the trader leverages observation, intuition, and probability to navigate the fog of the market.

Probabilistic Thinking in Action

Effective decision-making under uncertainty relies on assessing probabilities rather than seeking absolute certainties:

- **Range of Outcomes:** Identify multiple plausible scenarios for market movement, from best-case to worst-case, and assign subjective probabilities.
- **Weighted Decisions:** Base trades on expected value rather than certainty; actions should reflect both probability and potential impact.
- **Dynamic Adjustment:** Update probabilities in real-time as new information emerges, maintaining flexibility without succumbing to indecision.

Exercises for Practicing Decision-Making Under Uncertainty

Exercise 1: Scenario Probabilities For each trade, write down at least three possible outcomes with estimated probabilities. Act according to the expected value rather than attempting to predict a single outcome. Over time, this reinforces probabilistic reasoning and reduces emotional overreaction to unexpected movements.

Exercise 2: Decision Reflection Journal After executing trades, record your thought process:

- Which probabilities did you estimate accurately, and which did you misjudge?
- Did emotional responses influence your decisions under uncertainty?
- How did intuition align with conscious analysis?

This reflective practice strengthens awareness of biases and refines the integration of perception and probability.

Exercise 3: Controlled Simulations Engage in market simulations with multiple plausible outcomes, adjusting positions iteratively as probabilities shift. This builds skill in making adaptive decisions without relying on certainty, mirroring real-market dynamics.

Integrating Awareness, Probability, and Action

Advanced traders approach uncertainty through a triad:

1. **Awareness:** Observe markets and internal states without premature judgment.
2. **Probabilistic Assessment:** Evaluate likelihoods, risk-reward ratios, and scenario interdependencies.
3. **Conscious Action:** Make deliberate, flexible decisions aligned with the probabilistic landscape and personal risk tolerance.

This integration forms a feedback loop: heightened awareness refines probability estimates, informed probabilities guide action, and reflective evaluation strengthens both awareness and judgment.

Philosophical Perspective

Decision-making under uncertainty is an exercise in humility and presence. It requires acknowledging the limits of knowledge, embracing ambiguity, and trusting a disciplined process that blends intuition, observation, and probabilistic reasoning. Traders who act with clarity amid uncertainty cultivate resilience, adaptability, and the capacity to perceive opportunity where others see risk.

Closing Thought

Markets will always be uncertain. Success is not achieved by eliminating uncertainty but by navigating it with conscious awareness, probabilistic insight, and disciplined action. Advanced traders learn to perceive uncertainty not as a void to fear, but as a canvas upon which skill, intuition, and deliberate judgment can create structured, adaptive, and profitable responses. In embracing uncertainty, traders transform it from an obstacle into a partner, guiding decisions with both wisdom and flexibility in the ever-shifting landscape of the market.

Chapter 8

Time, Perception, and Flow

In the dynamic environment of financial markets, time is not merely a linear sequence of events it is a subjective experience shaped by attention, perception, and cognitive engagement. The perception of time influences how traders process information, react to price movements, and synchronize with market rhythms. Flow states, where awareness, intuition, and action converge seamlessly, allow traders to align with the probabilistic waves of the market, making decisions with clarity and precision under pressure.

This chapter explores the subjective nature of time in high-stakes trading, the concept of flow as a state of optimal engagement with market probabilities, and practical techniques to accelerate conscious awareness. By understanding and cultivating these dynamics, traders can enhance their situational perception, improve decision speed and accuracy, and navigate uncertainty with greater adaptive intelligence.

8.1 Subjectivity of Time in High-Pressure Decisions

Time is a construct that we often take for granted in our daily lives, yet in the high-stakes environment of financial markets, its perception can be profoundly subjective. Seconds can stretch into eternities during a sudden market crash, or hours can pass unnoticed when trading flows harmoniously. Understanding the malleability of perceived time is crucial for advanced traders because it directly affects attention, decision-making speed, and the ability to act effectively under pressure.

The Elastic Nature of Time

Neuroscience and cognitive psychology reveal that our experience of time is intimately linked to attention and emotional intensity. High-pressure situations, such as volatile price swings, trigger heightened arousal, which can dilate perceived time. Conversely, prolonged focus and deep engagement in routine analysis may compress perceived time, leading to a sense of flow where hours pass unnoticed.

Analogy: Imagine standing at the edge of a cliff, poised to leap into the unknown. Every heartbeat feels amplified, moments seem to stretch endlessly, and every decision carries immediate consequences. In contrast, when engrossed in a creative task, time dissolves, and the mind navigates complexity effortlessly. Market conditions create similar psychological landscapes: volatility expands time, flow contracts it, and traders must navigate both dimensions with awareness.

Impact on Decision-Making

Time perception influences cognitive processing in several critical ways:

- **Reaction Timing:** Overestimating or underestimating the passage of time can lead to premature or delayed trade execution.
- **Attention Allocation:** Temporal distortion affects which cues are noticed or ignored, influencing probabilistic assessments.
- **Emotional Calibration:** Heightened arousal can amplify fear or greed, biasing decisions if not consciously moderated.

Traders who recognize the subjectivity of time can better calibrate their mental states, balancing urgency with clarity, and action with reflection.

Practical Exercises

Exercise 1: Time Awareness Drills

1. Set a timer for random intervals between 30 seconds to 5 minutes.
2. During this interval, focus on observing market data without taking any action.
3. At the end, record your subjective estimate of elapsed time versus actual time.
4. Reflect on factors that influenced your perception: emotional intensity, concentration, or market volatility.

Exercise 2: Controlled Stress Simulation

1. Simulate a volatile market scenario using historical data or paper trading.
2. Track how quickly you process information and execute decisions.
3. Compare your decision speed and accuracy under pressure to calmer conditions.
4. Identify cognitive distortions caused by perceived time dilation or compression.

Exercise 3: Mindful Temporal Observation

1. Practice short meditation or breath-awareness sessions before trading.
2. Observe your internal sense of time passing without distraction.
3. This cultivates awareness of temporal perception and anchors attention, reducing the likelihood of overreacting to transient market movements.

Philosophical Perspective

Time is not merely a metric; it is a lens through which traders interpret reality. By acknowledging its subjectivity, traders gain access to a higher-order awareness where decisions are guided not only by data but also by mindful observation of their own perception. This perspective fosters patience amid chaos, presence in high-pressure moments, and the ability to synchronize actions with market dynamics rather than reacting impulsively.

Closing Thought

The mastery of temporal perception is a form of cognitive leverage. Traders who cultivate awareness of time's elasticity enhance their probabilistic reasoning, emotional regulation, and situational responsiveness. In the ever-shifting currents of the market, understanding and aligning with the subjective nature of time allows one to navigate volatility with composure, adaptivity, and a profound sense of presence. By internalizing the fluidity of time, advanced traders transform the market from a frenetic sequence of events into a dynamic field of probabilistic opportunities, ready to be observed, assessed, and acted upon with clarity.

8.2 Flow States as Alignment with Market Probability Waves

In the midst of market complexity, there exists a rare and precious state in which awareness, perception, and action converge seamlessly: flow. Flow is more than just heightened focus it is a cognitive resonance with the underlying probabilistic currents of the market. When a trader enters flow, decisions emerge effortlessly, probabilities are assessed intuitively, and action aligns harmoniously with the evolving dynamics of price and sentiment.

Understanding Flow in Trading

Flow, a concept popularized by psychologist Mihaly Csikszentmihalyi, describes a state of optimal engagement where challenge meets skill. In markets, flow manifests as a heightened sense of presence where the trader perceives subtle cues across timeframes, anticipates market microstructures, and responds fluidly without hesitation.

Analogy: Consider a surfer riding an ocean wave. The wave represents a probabilistic landscape: currents, swells, and winds create a dynamic, ever-changing environment. The surfer does not control the wave but attunes to it, predicting its movement through observation, experience, and intuition. Similarly, the trader in flow senses the probabilistic "waves" of the market, adjusting posture and position with subtle, informed shifts.

Flow and Probability Alignment

Markets are not deterministic; each price level is a node of probabilistic potential shaped by collective behavior, liquidity, and sentiment. Flow allows traders to perceive these probabilities with heightened clarity:

- **Intuitive Probabilistic Assessment:** Without conscious calculation, a trader senses which outcomes are more likely based on market rhythm, pattern, and volume.
- **Adaptive Response:** Decisions are made in real-time, continuously updating as the probability landscape shifts.
- **Emotional Coherence:** Emotional responses are balanced, preventing impulsive reactions and maintaining alignment with probabilistic reasoning.

Practical Exercises to Enter Flow

Exercise 1: Micro-Observation Practice

1. During a trading session, focus on a single instrument or timeframe.
2. Observe price movement, order flow, and volume changes for 10–15 minutes without executing trades.
3. Notice subtle patterns, anomalies, or rhythm shifts.
4. Reflect on the probabilistic possibilities these observations suggest.

Exercise 2: Synchronization Drill

1. Choose a historically volatile period or simulate live market data.
2. Practice aligning your decision-making pace with the market's tempo: when the market accelerates, move faster; when it slows, calibrate patience.
3. Record instances where timing and action harmonize with market movement.

Exercise 3: Mental Imagery of Probability Waves

1. Visualize market probabilities as waves of varying amplitude and frequency.
2. Mentally ride these waves, imagining how decisions would align with peaks, troughs, and oscillations.
3. Translate these visualizations into real-world trade scenarios, noting improved reaction times and clarity.

Narrative Insight

Advanced traders often describe flow as a sense of "being one with the market." It is not mystical; it is the alignment of conscious awareness, trained intuition, and probabilistic reasoning. Those who cultivate flow consistently report reduced stress, improved accuracy, and heightened confidence in decision-making.

Example: A seasoned trader in the foreign exchange market, after years of pattern recognition and adaptive practice, notices a subtle imbalance in EUR/USD liquidity. Without analytical deliberation, she adjusts her position just as the market begins to react, capturing a favorable move that would have been missed without alignment with the probabilistic wave.

Philosophical Perspective

Flow embodies the union of mind and market. It is a state where probabilities are perceived directly, decisions arise naturally, and the trader experiences both freedom and discipline. Flow transcends the reactive mindset, allowing the trader to act from a place of observation, resonance, and intuitive understanding.

Closing Reflection

Mastery in trading is not only about knowledge of instruments or technical analysis it is the capacity to enter and sustain flow, perceiving the probabilistic currents of the market with clarity. By practicing micro-observation, synchronization, and mental visualization of probability waves, traders cultivate a state where awareness, probability assessment, and action converge. In this alignment, trading becomes not just a technical endeavor but a conscious, adaptive dialogue with the market's inherent uncertainty, transforming complexity into opportunity and insight.

8.3 Techniques for Accelerated Conscious Awareness

In trading, the edge often lies not in access to more data, but in the depth of awareness brought to each observation and decision. Conscious awareness the ability to perceive, interpret, and act with clarity in real-time amplifies a trader's probabilistic reasoning, emotional calibration, and adaptive response. Accelerating this awareness is less about speed and more about cultivating a heightened sensitivity to market signals, cognitive biases, and internal states, allowing one to operate with both precision and presence.

The Role of Conscious Awareness in Trading

Awareness serves as the bridge between perception and action. Markets present infinite streams of information price ticks, order flows, news, and sentiment but not all of it is relevant. Without conscious calibration, traders can fall into reactive patterns, succumbing to fear, greed, or inertia. By deliberately training conscious awareness, one transforms observation into insight and probabilistic understanding into adaptive action.

Analogy: Imagine standing in a dense forest. Without awareness, the landscape is a blur: every tree, rustle, and shadow merges into noise. With focused attention, you perceive pathways, subtle changes in light, and the patterns of wildlife, allowing you to navigate effectively. Similarly, in markets, heightened awareness filters noise, revealing the underlying probabilistic structure.

Techniques to Cultivate Accelerated Awareness

1. Mindful Observation Drills

1. Allocate a fixed window during trading to observe a single market without executing trades.
2. Track micro-movements, order book shifts, and volume anomalies.
3. Record your observations and reflect on patterns or emergent behaviors.
4. Goal: Strengthen the capacity to notice subtle market cues without immediate reaction.

2. Breath-Anchoring for Focused Perception

1. Before entering a trading session, practice deep, rhythmic breathing for 2–5 minutes.

2. Use each exhale to release tension and each inhale to heighten sensory awareness.
3. While trading, periodically return to breath awareness to reset cognitive load and maintain clarity under pressure.

3. Probabilistic Visualization Exercises

1. Visualize multiple potential market scenarios as dynamic, overlapping probability clouds.
2. Mentally simulate decisions and consequences across these clouds.
3. Observe emotional reactions to each scenario, noting where fear, hope, or attachment may distort judgment.

4. Temporal Awareness Training

1. Engage in time-perception exercises by estimating intervals without a clock, comparing subjective and objective time.
2. Notice how market volatility or attention lapses alter your temporal perception.
3. This practice sharpens the ability to act promptly without rushing, calibrating decisions with market rhythm.

5. Reflective Journaling for Meta-Awareness

1. After each session, document not only trades and outcomes but also your cognitive and emotional states.
2. Identify patterns where awareness lapses led to suboptimal decisions.
3. Over time, journaling cultivates meta-cognition the awareness of your own mental processes which accelerates conscious adaptation.

Narrative Insight

Advanced traders often describe moments of clarity as a form of "expanded awareness," where multiple streams of information and probabilities converge effortlessly in the mind. This is not magic; it is the result of deliberate practice in observing patterns, managing attention, and integrating internal and external signals. By engaging in structured awareness exercises, traders train their minds to operate at higher resolution, detecting subtle market shifts before they manifest in price.

Example: A trader in commodities markets notices an unusual accumulation of bid orders across several correlated assets. Because of practiced conscious awareness, she recognizes the pattern as an early indicator of potential supply disruption. Her ability to perceive this probabilistic signal before it triggers widespread reaction allows her to position strategically with confidence and composure.

Philosophical Perspective

Conscious awareness is not merely a technique it is a state of being in which observation, intuition, and reflection coalesce. Markets, in all their probabilistic complexity, mirror the mind: clarity emerges when attention is trained, biases are acknowledged, and perception is refined. Accelerating awareness is a form of cognitive empowerment, enabling the trader to navigate uncertainty with deliberate insight rather than reactive instinct.

Closing Reflection

Techniques for accelerated conscious awareness transform trading from a reactive endeavor into a deliberate, adaptive practice. Through mindful observation, breath-anchoring, probabilistic visualization, temporal training, and reflective journaling, traders cultivate a heightened sensitivity to market dynamics, internal states, and emergent patterns. The conscious trader perceives opportunity in complexity, harmonizes action with probability, and maintains clarity amidst volatility ultimately converting awareness into actionable intelligence, and uncertainty into a field of strategic possibilities.

Chapter 9

Quantum Emotions

Emotions are often viewed as obstacles in trading forces that cloud judgment and disrupt rational decision-making. Yet, when understood through the lens of probabilistic markets and conscious awareness, emotions can be reframed as dynamic signals, influencing perception, attention, and the assessment of probabilities. This chapter explores the concept of *quantum emotions*, where feelings are not merely reactive but interact with the trader's cognitive framework, creating interference patterns that can either distort or enhance probabilistic reasoning.

We will examine how fear, greed, and hope act as modulators of perception, the ways in which emotional interference manifests in decision-making, and practical exercises to calibrate emotional states. By learning to observe, interpret, and harmonize emotions, traders can transform them from sources of bias into instruments of insight, aligning mental, emotional, and probabilistic flow for more coherent and adaptive market engagement.

9.1 Emotional Interference in Probabilistic Thinking

Trading is not a purely rational exercise; it is an intimate dialogue between perception, cognition, and emotion. In probabilistic markets, where outcomes are uncertain and patterns fluid, emotions act like subtle forces that warp the mind's probability calculations. Fear may exaggerate perceived risk, greed can inflate expectations of reward, and hope may blind a trader to alternative scenarios. Understanding these emotional interference patterns is essential for advanced traders seeking mastery over both the market and themselves.

The Quantum Nature of Emotions in Trading

Just as quantum particles exist in superpositions until observed, market probabilities fluctuate until a decision collapses them into an outcome. Emotions function similarly: they interact with cognitive processes, creating interference that can either reinforce or distort judgment. A spike in anxiety may amplify the perceived likelihood of adverse events, while excitement may increase overconfidence in favorable outcomes. Recognizing that emotions are dynamic, context-sensitive, and inseparable from perception allows traders to engage with them consciously rather than reactively.

Analogy: Imagine observing two overlapping waves in water. The peaks and troughs can amplify each other (constructive interference) or cancel each other out (destructive interference). Emotions act as these waves on cognitive perception fear, hope, and greed overlap with rational analysis, shaping how probabilities are evaluated. The trader who can map and modulate these emotional "waves" gains clarity in probabilistic thinking, much like a physicist controlling interference in an experiment.

Manifestations of Emotional Interference

- **Overestimation of Rare Events:** Fear of extreme loss can distort the assessment of probability, leading to overly conservative positions.
- **Underestimation of Risk:** Greed or euphoria may inflate the perceived probability of success, causing traders to take excessive exposure.
- **Confirmation Bias:** Hope can make traders selectively notice information that supports their desired outcome while ignoring contrary signals.
- **Emotional Momentum:** Past gains or losses can induce a cascade effect, influencing probability estimates in subsequent decisions.

Practical Exercises for Awareness

Exercise 1: Emotional Logging

1. During each trading session, record your emotional state at key decision points.
2. Note the market conditions, your perception of probabilities, and the decisions taken.
3. Reflect on patterns where emotion skewed your judgment, identifying triggers for interference.

Exercise 2: Probability Calibration

1. For each trade or market observation, assign a probability to potential outcomes before and after noticing emotional shifts.
2. Compare these estimates to actual market movements.

3. Over time, this trains recognition of how emotional states distort probabilistic thinking and reinforces objective assessment skills.

Exercise 3: Constructive Interference

1. Identify emotions that can enhance perception, such as curiosity or cautious optimism.

2. Consciously cultivate these states before analysis or decision-making.

3. Observe how these positive emotional waves interact with cognitive processing, amplifying clarity and insight rather than biasing probability assessment.

Philosophical Reflection

Emotions are not inherently adversarial to trading; they are integral to the probabilistic landscape. The goal is not to eliminate emotion but to understand and integrate it, recognizing its patterns and using it to enhance rather than distort perception. A trader who views emotions as dynamic variables interacting, interfering, and modulating probability estimates transforms what was once a source of bias into a sophisticated tool for adaptive decision-making.

Closing Thought

Emotional interference in probabilistic thinking is unavoidable, yet it is not insurmountable. By observing, mapping, and modulating emotions, traders can refine their perception of probabilities, align decisions with market realities, and navigate uncertainty with composed awareness. Mastery lies not in emotionless calculation but in conscious engagement with the full spectrum of human experience where mind, heart, and market probabilities converge in deliberate, insightful action.

9.2 Managing Fear, Greed, and Hope

In trading, fear, greed, and hope are the most potent emotional forces, subtly shaping perception, biasing probability assessment, and influencing decision-making. These emotions are not merely psychological obstacles they are signals from the mind-body system, reflecting how we interpret uncertainty and risk. The advanced trader does not suppress these feelings but understands, calibrates, and harnesses them, transforming raw emotion into informed action.

Fear: The Amplifier of Risk

Fear alerts us to potential danger, a deeply ingrained survival mechanism. In markets, fear can amplify perceived probabilities of adverse outcomes, causing traders to hesitate, exit prematurely, or avoid opportunities. Yet fear also has constructive potential: it can sharpen focus, enhance vigilance, and highlight hidden risks.

Exercise: Fear Mapping

1. Before each trade, rate your fear on a scale from 1 to 10.
2. Note what specific risk or uncertainty triggers this fear.
3. Visualize the worst-case outcome, then objectively assign a probability to its occurrence.
4. Decide on a pre-planned action based on this probability, not the intensity of fear.

By externalizing and quantifying fear, traders convert an emotional wave into a measurable signal for probabilistic reasoning.

Greed: The Distorter of Probability

Greed magnifies potential rewards, often leading to overconfidence, excessive position sizing, or ignoring contrary signals. It creates a bias toward favorable outcomes and inflates the subjective probability of success. Harnessed consciously, greed can motivate disciplined pursuit of opportunity while avoiding reckless overextension.

Exercise: Reward-Risk Calibration

1. Before entering a trade, calculate objective risk-reward ratios and probability weighted outcomes.
2. Compare your intuitive excitement with these calculations.
3. Adjust position size and exposure to align with probabilistic assessment rather than emotional desire.

Through this alignment, greed transforms from a distorting impulse into a driver for disciplined opportunity.

Hope: The Bias of Expectation

Hope colors expectations, creating selective attention toward confirming evidence while ignoring contrary signals. While hope can sustain morale during drawdowns, unexamined hope introduces bias into probability judgments and decision-making.

Exercise: Probability Reality Check

1. Identify situations where hope is influencing your perception of outcomes.

2. List evidence supporting the desired outcome and evidence against it.

3. Assign probabilities to both scenarios and make decisions based on objective assessment rather than desire.

By converting hope into conscious probability evaluation, traders preserve optimism without compromising judgment.

Integrated Emotional Calibration

Managing fear, greed, and hope requires a holistic approach:

- **Observation:** Recognize emotions as they arise, labeling them without judgment.

- **Quantification:** Assign scales or probabilities to emotional intensity to integrate them into decision frameworks.

- **Alignment:** Adjust positions, timing, or exposure to reconcile emotional state with rational probability assessment.

- **Reflection:** Maintain a journal tracking emotional triggers, their impact on decisions, and corrective strategies applied.

Narrative Insight

Consider a trader during a volatile earnings announcement. Fear spikes as price moves against a position, greed surges with a potential breakout, and hope clings to favorable outcomes. Instead of reacting impulsively, a calibrated approach would involve pausing, acknowledging each emotion, quantifying risk, and taking action aligned with probabilistic assessment. The result: disciplined trades, reduced emotional interference, and enhanced confidence in navigating uncertainty.

Philosophical Perspective

Emotions in trading are neither enemies nor mere distractions they are integral elements of probabilistic perception. By understanding and managing fear, greed, and hope, traders cultivate emotional coherence, allowing them to perceive probabilities more accurately and act with deliberate intent. This mastery is not about suppressing human experience but integrating it, creating a mental ecosystem where perception, probability, and emotion coexist in harmony.

Closing Reflection

The conscious trader transforms fear, greed, and hope into instruments of insight. Through awareness, quantification, and reflection, emotions are calibrated rather than repressed, guiding probability-informed decisions. In this interplay of mind, heart, and market, emotional mastery becomes a catalyst for clarity, adaptability, and sustainable trading performance, turning uncertainty into a canvas for strategic, conscious action.

9.3 Emotional Calibration Drills

Mastery of markets requires more than technical knowledge or probabilistic reasoning; it demands mastery over the mind that perceives and interprets probabilities. Emotions fear, greed, hope, frustration, and excitement act as both lenses and filters, shaping how traders interpret market signals. Without calibration, emotions distort probabilities, bias decisions, and erode composure. Through deliberate drills, traders can train their emotional system to respond coherently, enhancing awareness, intuition, and probabilistic alignment.

The Philosophy of Emotional Calibration

Emotional calibration is the art of aligning inner states with external uncertainty. It does not mean suppressing feelings but recognizing their influence, observing their fluctuations, and modulating intensity to maintain clarity in decision-making. Like tuning a musical instrument before performance, calibration ensures that the mind's perception resonates harmoniously with market dynamics.

Analogy: Consider a sailboat navigating stormy seas. The wind and waves are external forces; the sailor's skill lies not in eliminating them but in adjusting sails, tension, and rudder to harness energy efficiently. Similarly, the trader learns to channel emotional currents rather than resist them, converting internal turbulence into adaptive insight.

Drill 1: Real-Time Emotional Labeling

1. During each trading session, pause periodically to observe and name the dominant emotion: "fear," "greed," "hope," "frustration," or "curiosity."
2. Rate intensity on a 1–10 scale.
3. Reflect on how this emotion influences your perception of probabilities or decision tendencies.
4. Adjust position sizing or exposure accordingly, reinforcing the habit of conscious, rather than reactive, trading.

Drill 2: Probability-Emotion Mapping

1. Select a set of potential trades or market scenarios.

2. Assign subjective probabilities to outcomes based on objective analysis.

3. Simultaneously note the emotional response to each probability estimate.

4. Analyze where emotion inflates or deflates perceived likelihood, and recalibrate to align subjective perception with probabilistic reasoning.

Drill 3: Emotional Reset Anchors

1. Identify physical or mental anchors breathing, posture, or a brief mindfulness cue that reliably reduce emotional intensity.

2. Practice activating the anchor during simulated stress scenarios, such as rapid price swings or unexpected news events.

3. Incorporate the anchor into live trading, ensuring that heightened emotion does not override probabilistic assessment.

Drill 4: Scenario Visualization with Emotional Forecasting

1. Mentally simulate multiple market outcomes, including best-case, worst-case, and neutral scenarios.

2. For each scenario, anticipate emotional responses and pre-plan behavioral strategies.

3. This exercise strengthens the ability to maintain composure across diverse probabilistic landscapes, effectively creating a "mental rehearsal" for high-stakes decisions.

Drill 5: Reflective Journaling for Emotional Patterns

1. After each trading session, document not only trades and outcomes but also the emotional states present at key decision points.

2. Identify recurring triggers, interference patterns, and moments when calibration succeeded or failed.

3. Over time, this practice builds meta-awareness, allowing the trader to anticipate emotional reactions before they manifest.

Narrative Insight

Advanced traders often describe emotional calibration as the difference between reactive chaos and adaptive flow. One trader, facing a sudden market reversal, noticed an immediate spike in fear. Instead of exiting impulsively, she activated her breathing anchor, mentally reviewed probability-weighted scenarios, and adjusted position exposure calmly. The result: a decision aligned with probabilistic assessment, rather than emotional reflex, yielding both a strategic advantage and emotional resilience.

Philosophical Reflection

Emotions are inseparable from consciousness and perception; attempting to eliminate them is futile and counterproductive. Calibration transforms these intrinsic forces into instruments of insight. By systematically observing, labeling, modulating, and reflecting on emotions, traders harmonize internal states with market probabilities, creating coherence between mind, emotion, and action.

Closing Thoughts

Emotional calibration drills provide actionable, repeatable frameworks for mastering the human component of trading. Through labeling, mapping, anchoring, visualization, and journaling, traders cultivate resilience, clarity, and adaptive intelligence. In probabilistic markets, where uncertainty is constant, emotional calibration is not optional it is an essential skill for conscious, effective, and sustainable trading performance. By training the mind to perceive with clarity, act with intentionality, and respond with equilibrium, traders convert emotional energy from a source of interference into a conduit for insight and strategic advantage.

Chapter 10

The Trader as Observer and Creator

Markets are often treated as external, objective entities vast, impersonal systems responding to economic data, policy shifts, and news events. Yet, from a probabilistic and consciousness-informed perspective, the trader is never merely a spectator. Every observation, every decision, subtly shapes market dynamics, creating a feedback loop between perception and reality.

This chapter explores the dual role of the trader as both observer and creator. Drawing from the concept of the observer effect, it highlights how awareness, attention, and intention influence market behavior, not just at a psychological level but through collective interactions among participants. Traders learn that conscious perception can align with probabilities, while unexamined biases can amplify volatility and mispricing.

10.1 The Observer Effect in Market Dynamics

In quantum physics, the observer effect describes how the mere act of observation can influence the state of a system. In financial markets, a similar phenomenon occurs: traders' perceptions, decisions, and actions ripple through the market, subtly influencing outcomes and shaping probability distributions. The observer is not detached; they are an active participant in the creation of market reality.

Conceptual Foundations

Every market participant interprets information, forms expectations, and acts based on subjective judgment. Orders placed, positions adjusted, and sentiments expressed collectively alter supply-demand dynamics, liquidity, and volatility. Even the act of observing a price chart or reading a news update is filtered through perception, prior beliefs, and emotional states, which then guide action. In this sense, observation and creation are intertwined the trader observes the market, interprets it through a probabilistic lens, and simultaneously participates in the unfolding reality.

Analogy: Imagine a pond where every stone thrown creates ripples. An observer standing at the edge sees these ripples and infers patterns of movement. But the observer also picks up a stone and tosses it in, creating new waves that alter the very patterns they sought to understand. Similarly, in markets, awareness is never neutral; every action subtly modifies the environment, generating feedback loops that shape probabilities.

Narrative Insight

Consider a professional trader analyzing a sudden spike in trading volume in a cryptocurrency. Her initial observation triggers a cascade of mental simulations: "Is this a pump orchestrated by whales? Is it news-driven? Are my peers reacting similarly?" Each micro-decision entering a position, hedging exposure, or choosing to observe contributes to the probabilistic state of the market. Other traders, observing the same spike, respond in ways that reinforce or counteract her interpretation. The market becomes a tapestry of interwoven intentions, a dynamic system co-created by multiple conscious observers.

Practical Reflection

To operationalize the observer effect in trading:

1. **Pause Before Acting:** Recognize that your actions will influence probabilities. Take a moment to assess whether your response is aligned with probabilistic reasoning or reactive impulse.

2. **Observe Without Judgment:** Track market movements objectively, noting probabilities and potential outcomes without immediate emotional labeling. This reduces interference from preconceptions and biases.

3. **Reflect on Feedback Loops:** After trades, analyze how your actions contributed to shifts in market behavior. Identify patterns of influence and unintended consequences.

4. **Simulate Observer Scenarios:** Mentally place yourself in multiple roles observer, participant, and analyst to understand the interplay of attention, expectation, and market response.

Exercises for Observer Alignment

1. **Market Journaling:** Record observations, interpretations, actions, and resulting market movements. Note instances where your awareness may have contributed to market changes.

2. **Probability Adjustment Drill:** Observe a price move, estimate multiple potential outcomes with probabilities, and consciously act to align with these assessments. Compare actual market evolution with your probabilistic forecast.

3. **Mindful Observation Practice:** During volatile periods, practice maintaining calm, detached attention to the market. Observe without immediate execution, reflecting on how awareness alone influences perception and decision-making.

Philosophical Reflection

The observer effect reminds us that markets are not inert mechanisms but living systems infused with perception and intention. Conscious traders recognize their dual role: to perceive accurately and to act intentionally, understanding that observation itself alters probabilities. By cultivating mindful, reflective engagement, traders can navigate uncertainty with clarity, transforming observation from passive reception into a dynamic tool for conscious market participation.

Closing Thoughts

Advanced trading mastery requires embracing the observer effect not as a paradox to solve, but as a principle to embody. Through awareness, deliberate observation, and reflective practice, traders align perception, probability, and action, co-creating market realities while maintaining composure and strategic clarity. In the interplay between mind and market, every act of observation becomes an act of creation.

10.2 Co-Creation Between Mind and Market

Markets are often portrayed as external, objective arenas vast ecosystems where prices respond to data, news, and economic forces. Yet, beneath this surface lies a more intricate truth: each trader's mind participates in the ongoing creation of market reality. Perception shapes action, and action feeds back into the market, subtly altering probabilities, liquidity, and sentiment. In essence, markets are co-created by the collective cognition of all participants.

Conceptual Foundations

Co-creation is the principle that traders are both observers and contributors to market dynamics. Every decision whether to enter a position, hedge risk, or remain passive interacts with the probabilities of future price movements.

Traders' expectations and interpretations influence collective behavior, forming feedback loops that drive trends, reversals, and anomalies. Unlike classical deterministic models, where markets "move on their own," co-creation recognizes the interdependence between conscious minds and probabilistic outcomes.

Analogy: Imagine a jazz ensemble improvising together. Each musician listens, interprets, and responds in real time, creating a piece that emerges from collective input. No single player controls the outcome, yet each contributes to the evolving melody. Markets operate similarly: the price "music" emerges from countless traders observing, interpreting, and acting in tandem.

Narrative Insight

Consider a trader observing a sudden rally in a tech stock. Her probabilistic assessment suggests that the move may be overextended, yet the visible enthusiasm of peers triggers subtle anticipation. Deciding to participate cautiously, she places a measured buy order. Combined with hundreds of other traders making similar assessments, this collective action reinforces the probability structure of the market, shaping the rally itself. Her mind did not simply witness the event; it became part of the emergent pattern.

Practical Reflection

To harness co-creation consciously, traders can adopt several practices:

1. **Mindful Engagement:** Before acting, pause to recognize your influence on the probabilistic landscape. Ask, "How does my perception and action contribute to market dynamics?"

2. **Probability-Aware Decision-Making:** Align trades with probabilistic assessments rather than reactive impulses. Consider the potential feedback your action may trigger.

3. **Scenario Simulation:** Mentally model multiple trader responses to your anticipated action. Visualize how collective behavior could evolve from your participation.

4. **Adaptive Observation:** Continuously monitor the evolving probabilities, adjusting positions while maintaining awareness of your role in shaping outcomes.

Exercises for Conscious Co-Creation

1. **Observer-Participant Journaling:** Record moments when your trades influenced broader market behavior. Reflect on how conscious awareness could have enhanced alignment with probabilistic forecasts.

2. **Feedback Loop Mapping:** Identify patterns where your action reinforced or counteracted market trends. Map these interactions to understand co-creation dynamics.

3. **Simulated Market Influence Drill:** In a controlled trading simulation, consciously vary your orders and observe how market responses shift. Analyze which actions produced coherent alignment with probabilistic expectations.

Philosophical Reflection

Co-creation challenges the illusion of detachment. Markets are neither fully external nor entirely internal; they exist in the interplay between mind and collective reality. Conscious traders embrace this duality, recognizing that perception, intention, and probabilistic reasoning are inseparable from outcomes. By participating mindfully, traders transform uncertainty from a source of anxiety into a medium for strategic influence.

Closing Thoughts

Understanding markets as co-created systems empowers traders to operate with awareness, intentionality, and adaptability. Each observation and action becomes a contribution to the emergent probability landscape, enhancing both clarity and control. By integrating perception, probability, and conscious action, advanced traders navigate complex markets not as passive spectators, but as active, responsible co-creators of evolving financial realities.

10.3 Practical Exercises for Observer Alignment

Awareness alone is insufficient without disciplined practice. To internalize the principles of observation and co-creation, traders must engage in exercises that reinforce conscious alignment between perception, probability, and action. These exercises are designed to cultivate meta-awareness, enhance probabilistic reasoning, and strengthen the trader's capacity to act deliberately in complex market environments.

Exercise 1: Observation Journaling

1. During every trading session, record your observations of market events, including price movements, volume changes, and emerging patterns.

2. Note your immediate perceptions and emotional reactions fear, excitement, curiosity, or doubt.

3. Reflect on how these observations influenced subsequent decisions.

4. Over time, analyze recurring patterns of bias or reactive tendencies, identifying opportunities for greater alignment with probabilistic reasoning.

Reflection Tip: Compare your subjective perception of events with actual market outcomes. This practice reveals blind spots and strengthens conscious observation.

Exercise 2: Probability-Weighted Decision Simulation

1. Select a recent or simulated market scenario.

2. Assign subjective probabilities to several potential outcomes based on both quantitative data and qualitative intuition.

3. Before taking any action, pause and visualize each outcome unfolding. Consider how your decision may influence probabilities.

4. Take a measured action aligned with the most probable scenario, then observe how the market responds.

5. Record discrepancies between anticipated and actual outcomes to refine probabilistic awareness.

Analogy: Think of a chess player anticipating an opponent's moves. Every observation informs a probability-weighted prediction, guiding strategic action while remaining adaptive to evolving conditions.

Exercise 3: Mindful Market Observation

1. During volatile or high-pressure periods, practice detached observation without immediate execution.

2. Focus attention on patterns rather than individual price points. Observe order flow, liquidity changes, and clustering of market reactions.

3. Note emotional impulses as they arise, acknowledging them without judgment.

4. Allow observation to inform decisions consciously rather than reactively.

Philosophical Insight: By separating perception from impulsive action, traders cultivate a "witnessing consciousness," which reduces interference from emotional noise and cognitive bias.

Exercise 4: Co-Creation Awareness Drill

1. Select a small position or paper trade in a live or simulated environment.

2. Before executing, reflect on how your trade might influence other participants' perceptions and market movement.

3. Execute the trade while maintaining conscious attention to feedback effects, noting both expected and unexpected market responses.

4. Afterward, review the session to identify how your awareness and actions contributed to the market's evolving probability landscape.

Narrative Example: A trader placing a small position during a thinly traded stock noticed a sudden shift in momentum after her order was executed. By recognizing her influence, she adapted position sizing and timing, maintaining alignment with probabilistic expectations rather than reacting purely to emergent price action.

Exercise 5: Reflective Meta-Analysis

1. At the end of each trading day or week, review both successful and suboptimal decisions.

2. Document which actions were guided by conscious observation versus reactive impulse.

3. Identify moments when awareness altered outcomes positively and moments where inattentiveness introduced errors.

4. Develop personalized strategies for reinforcing observer-aligned behavior in future sessions.

Practical Takeaway: The continuous cycle of observation, action, and reflection transforms trading from a reactive endeavor into a conscious, probability-informed practice.

Philosophical Reflection

Advanced traders understand that markets are living, probabilistic systems, and that their awareness directly shapes outcomes. Exercises in observer alignment cultivate the subtle interplay between perception and action, allowing traders to participate in the market with clarity, composure, and intentionality. Through disciplined journaling, simulation, mindfulness, co-creation drills, and meta-reflection, the observer becomes a conscious participant, bridging perception, probability, and strategic execution.

Closing Thoughts

Practical exercises are not abstract rituals they are the bridge between conceptual understanding and applied mastery. By integrating these exercises into daily trading practice, traders strengthen their capacity to perceive accurately, act intentionally, and co-create market outcomes. Observer alignment transforms uncertainty from a source of stress into a dynamic canvas for informed, deliberate, and adaptive decision-making.

Part III

Quantum Frameworks for Trading

Chapter 11

Probability-Driven Strategy Design

In probabilistic markets, strategy is not a fixed plan but a dynamic experiment a continuous engagement with uncertainty, feedback, and evolving probabilities. Traditional trading often emphasizes rigid rules, historical patterns, or deterministic signals. While these can provide structure, they risk neglecting the fluid, perception-dependent nature of markets. Probability-driven strategy design reframes trading as an iterative process of hypothesis, observation, and adaptation, where each trade serves as both an experiment and a data point in a larger probabilistic system.

This approach emphasizes that every position, order, and exposure interacts with the ever-shifting landscape of market probabilities. By consciously integrating probability assessment into strategy, traders align decision-making with the underlying uncertainty of market dynamics, reducing reactive behavior and enhancing adaptive intelligence.

11.1 Trades as Probability Experiments

Every trade is, at its core, an experiment. It is an interaction with uncertainty, a probe into the probabilistic landscape of the market, and a live test of the trader's assumptions, perception, and awareness. Viewing trades as probability experiments reframes the act of trading from a purely transactional pursuit to a reflective, iterative engagement with uncertainty. This perspective transforms each position into a source of learning, adaptation, and conscious alignment.

Conceptual Foundation

Traditional trading often treats signals, indicators, or patterns as deterministic triggers: buy when this occurs, sell when that happens. However, markets are not rigid machines; they are emergent systems shaped by countless interactions, perceptions, and feedback loops. By acknowledging that outcomes are probabilistic rather than certain, traders cultivate a mindset that emphasizes likelihoods, scenario planning, and iterative refinement.

Analogy: Consider a scientist testing a hypothesis. A single experiment rarely yields conclusive proof; it provides data, insights, and opportunities to adjust assumptions. Similarly, each trade informs the trader not just about price movement but about the accuracy of their perception, the responsiveness of the market, and their own cognitive biases.

Designing a Probabilistic Trade

A probability-driven trade begins with three key components:

1. **Hypothesis Formation:** Define why a trade should work. For instance, "If liquidity clusters near this price level, the probability of a rebound increases."
2. **Probability Assessment:** Assign subjective probabilities to possible outcomes upside, downside, or neutral based on analysis, pattern recognition, and market context.
3. **Risk Calibration:** Determine position sizing and exposure relative to the probability-weighted risk-reward profile. This ensures that potential loss is proportional to uncertainty rather than emotional conviction.

Narrative Insight

A seasoned trader recounts a day when a stock showed a bullish pattern. Rather than jumping in immediately, he treated the setup as an experiment. He defined three potential outcomes: a strong rebound (40% probability), a minor correction before upward continuation (35%), and a deeper decline (25%). With calibrated position sizing, he entered the trade, observing the market's response in real-time. As the market unfolded, he noted deviations from his expectations and adjusted his exposure, learning from each micro-movement without panic or overcommitment. By framing the trade as an experiment, he maintained composure, preserved capital, and refined his probabilistic intuition.

Exercises for Traders

1. **Scenario Mapping:** Before taking a trade, list 3–5 potential outcomes and assign subjective probabilities. Update these probabilities as the market evolves.
2. **Outcome Debriefing:** After each trade, compare actual outcomes with probability estimates. Note where perception aligned or diverged from reality.

3. **Iterative Adjustment:** Adjust position sizing, entry, or exit rules based on observed discrepancies between expected and actual outcomes. Treat each trade as a learning iteration.

4. **Meta-Reflection:** Maintain a trading journal that tracks not only outcomes but also emotional responses and cognitive biases encountered during the experiment.

Philosophical Reflection

Viewing trades as experiments encourages a mindset of humility, curiosity, and resilience. It shifts the focus from winning or losing in the short term to understanding, adaptation, and probabilistic mastery over the long term. The market becomes a laboratory, uncertainty becomes data, and the trader becomes a conscious participant in a dynamic system. Each trade, whether profitable or unprofitable, contributes to a deeper understanding of market behavior, personal cognition, and the intricate dance between perception and probability.

Closing Thoughts

Probability-driven trading is not about predicting the future with certainty. It is about embracing uncertainty as a guiding principle, designing trades as structured experiments, and using outcomes to refine both strategy and self-awareness. By treating every position as a probability experiment, traders cultivate composure, enhance intuition, and develop an adaptive mindset transforming uncertainty from a source of fear into a tool for strategic insight and conscious market mastery.

11.2 Risk-Reward as a Dynamic Wave Function

In classical trading thought, risk-reward is often treated as a static ratio: for example, a trade offers a potential gain of 3 units for every 1 unit of risk. While such a framework is useful for initial assessment, it fails to capture the fluid, probabilistic, and perception-dependent nature of modern markets. A dynamic approach treats risk and reward not as fixed points, but as a wave-like function, constantly modulated by market conditions, trader perception, and probabilistic outcomes.

Conceptual Foundation

Markets are living systems. Liquidity ebbs and flows, volatility surges and subsides, and trader behavior interacts in complex feedback loops. In this environment, the expected payoff of a trade is not a single, deterministic value; it is a spectrum of potential outcomes weighted by probability.

Analogy: Imagine standing on the shore of a turbulent ocean. Waves represent potential market moves. The height and timing of each wave are uncertain, yet a skilled surfer reads patterns, anticipates peaks, and positions themselves to ride the wave most effectively. Similarly, risk and reward in trading are not fixed heights but dynamic surfaces that fluctuate with probability, sentiment, and feedback.

Dynámic Wave Conceptualization

Consider the trade as a wave function:

- **Amplitude:** Represents potential magnitude of gain or loss. High amplitude implies high volatility; low amplitude indicates stability.
- **Frequency:** Captures how quickly probabilities shift as market data evolves. High-frequency markets require rapid recalibration.
- **Phase:** Encodes the alignment between market context, trader perception, and probability estimates. Misalignment increases exposure to unanticipated risk.

This visualization encourages traders to perceive risk-reward not as static, but as a living curve that must be continually observed, assessed, and adapted to.

Narrative Insight

Consider a trader monitoring an emerging technology stock. Traditional risk-reward analysis might suggest a fixed 2:1 ratio based on historical volatility. However, real-time market signals earnings sentiment, order flow, and collective trader behavior indicate that the probability distribution of outcomes has shifted. By conceptualizing risk-reward as a dynamic wave, the trader adjusts position size and stop levels, anticipating potential oscillations.

During the trade, the market moves erratically, testing stop levels and triggering emotional reactions. Yet the trader, observing the wave-like dynamics and probabilistic distribution of outcomes, maintains composure, modulates exposure, and aligns action with unfolding probabilities rather than static assumptions.

Exercises for Traders

1. **Wave Mapping:** Before entering a trade, sketch potential price movements as a probability wave, estimating likely highs, lows, and modes. Update the wave dynamically as market data arrives.

2. **Amplitude Adjustment:** Track volatility in real-time and adjust position size proportionally. Higher amplitude (volatility) warrants conservative exposure; lower amplitude allows greater participation.

3. **Phase Alignment Drill:** Compare subjective probability assessments with observed market conditions. Note where misalignment occurs and recalibrate position or strategy to minimize decoherence.

4. **Reflective Journaling:** After trading, document instances where dynamic risk-reward visualization influenced decision-making. Assess whether adjustments improved outcome alignment and probabilistic awareness.

Philosophical Reflection

Viewing risk-reward as a dynamic wave aligns trading with the fundamental probabilistic nature of markets. It encourages adaptability, continuous observation, and conscious alignment between perception and action. Traders who embrace this perspective recognize that certainty is an illusion; the market is a constantly evolving system of probabilities, and effective engagement requires fluidity, awareness, and responsiveness.

Closing Thoughts

By conceptualizing risk-reward as a dynamic, wave-like function, traders cultivate a mindset that anticipates change rather than reacts to it. They learn to ride market probabilities with skillful adaptability, modulate emotional responses, and align decision-making with probabilistic realities. In doing so, risk transforms from a source of anxiety into a navigable landscape, and reward emerges not as a fixed target but as the natural consequence of informed, conscious, and adaptive participation in the market's unfolding wave.

11.3 Case Applications

The theoretical frameworks of probability-driven trading dynamic risk-reward, wave functions, and observer-alignment come alive when applied to real-world scenarios. Case applications are not simply examples; they are laboratories for translating abstract concepts into conscious, probabilistic action. By examining historical trades, market events, and simulated exercises, traders can internalize principles, refine intuition, and bridge the gap between perception and execution.

Case Study 1: Volatility Compression and the Breakout Trade

Consider a technology stock consolidating within a tight range for several weeks. Traditional deterministic analysis might signal a breakout based purely on price patterns. However, a probabilistic trader views this as a dynamic system:

- The probability cloud of potential breakout directions is mapped, including likelihoods of false breakouts or range continuation.
- Emotional states are monitored anticipation, fear of missing out, and overconfidence may bias the trader toward impulsive entry.
- Dynamic risk-reward is assessed: stop levels are set relative to the amplitude of the volatility compression wave, adjusting position sizing according to real-time market data.

The result: when the breakout occurs, the trader enters with a calibrated position, prepared for both success and failure, and executes with awareness rather than reflex. Post-trade reflection strengthens probabilistic perception for future similar setups.

Case Study 2: Intermarket Correlation and Entangled Decisions

A trader managing multiple assets observes correlations between equity indices and commodity futures. Rather than assuming independence, the trader treats them as entangled systems:

- Probabilities of market moves in one asset are updated dynamically based on movements in correlated assets.
- Emotional interference, such as fear of loss in one market affecting decisions in another, is actively monitored and recalibrated.
- Scenario visualization is used to anticipate cascading outcomes, preparing for both amplifying and dampening effects of intermarket dynamics.

By treating correlations as live probability signals rather than static relationships, the trader navigates interconnected risks, maintaining coherent decision-making across multiple positions.

Case Study 3: News-Driven Probabilistic Assessment

High-impact economic news often triggers abrupt market shifts. Consider a central bank announcement on interest rates:

- A deterministic approach might simply react to headline direction.

- A probabilistic trader constructs multiple outcome states: rate hike larger than expected, as expected, or a dovish surprise.
- Emotional calibration drills are engaged observing the surge of fear or greed and preventing impulsive overreaction.
- Decision-making aligns with the weighted probabilities and risk-reward dynamics, rather than the immediate emotional impulse.

The trader enters positions scaled to probability-weighted expectations, ready to adapt if the market deviates from anticipated scenarios. This reflects conscious engagement with uncertainty rather than reactive guessing.

Practical Exercises

1. **Historical Replay Analysis:** Choose past trades or market events. Reconstruct the probability distributions that could have existed at the time and simulate decision-making using dynamic risk-reward frameworks.
2. **Entangled Asset Simulation:** Select correlated markets and practice updating probability clouds in real-time as one asset moves, noting the impact on others.
3. **Scenario Planning Drill:** For upcoming news or events, map multiple probabilistic outcomes and anticipate emotional reactions for each. Plan entry, exit, and risk management aligned with these probabilities.
4. **Reflective Journaling:** After live trades, document how the probabilistic frameworks influenced decision-making, highlighting moments of coherence or decoherence, emotional interference, and adaptation.

Philosophical Reflection

Case applications illuminate the inseparability of perception, probability, and consciousness in markets. Probabilistic frameworks are not rigid formulas but lenses for understanding uncertainty. Each trade, news event, or correlated move becomes an opportunity to observe the mind's influence on probability assessment and to cultivate alignment between awareness, emotion, and action.

Closing Thoughts

By engaging with case applications, traders move from abstract comprehension to actionable insight. They learn to:

- Map probability clouds in real-time.
- Anticipate emotional interference and calibrate responses.

- Align decisions with dynamic risk-reward and market-wave structures.
- Reflect systematically to internalize lessons and enhance future probabilistic perception.

These exercises transform understanding into skill, fostering a conscious, adaptive, and resilient approach to trading where every decision is informed, probabilistic, and harmonized with both internal awareness and external market dynamics.

Chapter 12

Feedback Loops and Quantum Cycles

Markets are not linear machines they are recursive organisms, pulsing with cycles of perception, reaction, and adaptation. Every price movement contains echoes of prior decisions; every decision becomes part of the next price movement. This is the essence of a feedback loop where cause and effect intertwine so tightly that they become indistinguishable, forming a continuous cycle of cognition and consequence.

In the quantum analogy, feedback loops represent the oscillation of probabilities through time. Just as particles exist in waves of superposition until observed, market probabilities fluctuate within dynamic cycles until traders act collapsing potential into price. The process repeats endlessly, each iteration shaped by new information, emotional resonance, and the evolving collective mind of the market.

Why feedback matters: In trading, perception does not merely interpret market reality it helps create it. When enough participants share a belief, their collective behavior amplifies that belief into price movement. Overconfidence inflates bubbles; fear accelerates crashes. Both arise not from randomness but from recursive loops feedback systems where thought influences action, and action reshapes thought.

Mental resonance and rhythm: Traders who thrive over time learn to tune their internal rhythms to the natural cycles of the market. They observe the expansions and contractions of volatility, the oscillation between euphoria and despair, and the waves of liquidity that flow through every session. Aligning mental models with these rhythms transforms trading from reactive engagement into fluid participation a dance between awareness and adaptation.

12.1 Recursive Market Patterns and Cognitive Feedback

The Loop Between Market and Mind

Markets are not mechanical systems governed solely by data or models they are recursive organisms that feed upon their own reflections. Every tick, price movement, and volatility expansion carries echoes of prior expectations and reactions. Traders do not respond to the market itself; they respond to their interpretation of how others might respond. Each interpretation becomes an input for the next, forming a continuous cognitive feedback loop.

The market, therefore, is not merely a pricing engine it is a mirror reflecting the collective psychology of its participants. Every surge of optimism or panic leaves a recursive imprint on price structure, shaping patterns that, in turn, shape future perceptions. To trade effectively is to perceive these loops not as linear cause-and-effect chains, but as self-referential dynamics of information and emotion.

Understanding Recursion: From Code to Cognition

In mathematics and computer science, *recursion* describes a process that references itself, where each output becomes the next input. Markets follow this same logic.

> Prices rise → traders interpret bullish signals → they buy → prices rise further.

This is a positive feedback loop amplification through confirmation.
At some saturation point, however, self-correction begins:

> Prices rise too fast → traders fear overextension → they sell → prices fall.

This becomes negative feedback stabilization through counteraction.

Just as natural systems oscillate between growth and equilibrium, market trends alternate between amplification and correction. These oscillations are the rhythmic pulse of the market expressions of collective emotion balancing between greed and fear, hope and doubt. Recognizing this rhythmic interplay allows traders to anticipate transitions between phases of acceleration and reversion.

The Cognitive Mirror

External feedback loops in markets find their mirror within the trader's own mind. Every decision generates emotional data confidence, regret, excitement, frustration which then alters future perception and behavior.

A profitable trade boosts confidence, often leading to increased risk-taking or selective perception. A loss triggers caution or revenge impulses, distorting judgment and compressing awareness. Over time, these emotional traces form internal feedback loops that bias probabilistic assessment.

The advanced trader must, therefore, learn to observe two interlocking systems:

1. The **external feedback loop**: market participants interacting and amplifying signals through collective behavior.
2. The **internal feedback loop**: emotions, beliefs, and expectations influencing the trader's own decision-making.

Mastery lies in recognizing how these loops synchronize and interfere. When internal emotion amplifies external volatility, perception collapses into reactivity. When awareness stabilizes, the trader perceives both systems clearly and acts coherently within uncertainty.

The Market as a Self-Referential Intelligence

Each trader observing the market also becomes part of what they observe. When many participants recognize the same pattern say, a "head and shoulders" formation their collective anticipation manifests in actual orders, stop placements, and exits. Observation becomes creation.

This is the **observer effect** in market dynamics: the act of perception alters the outcome. The chart becomes a map not of objective reality, but of shared expectation loops.

Thus, price is not a passive reflection of fundamentals it is an *aggregate projection of cognition*. The market evolves as a self-referential intelligence, continuously rewriting itself through feedback between observation and participation. Every trader, consciously or not, contributes to that rewriting.

Emotional Amplification and Entropy

Every recursive system risks runaway amplification. Bull markets accelerate as optimism fuels buying; bear markets spiral as fear amplifies selling. These cycles continue until emotional energy collective or individual reaches exhaustion, a state of psychological entropy. The bubble bursts, panic subsides, and negative feedback restores equilibrium.

For the conscious trader, this recognition transforms chaos into structure. Extremes are no longer viewed as anomalies but as logical outcomes of recursive amplification. Awareness of when emotion dominates feedback allows strategic detachment standing aside or fading extremes before the loop collapses.

Fractal Recursion: Patterns Within Patterns

Fractals, mathematical forms where the whole mirrors the parts, provide a visual metaphor for market recursion. Zoom into a five-minute chart and you will find the same formations trends, consolidations, reversals that appear on hourly or daily scales. Each timeframe is a microcosm of the same cognitive processes.

Why? Because the psychological forces driving behavior hope, fear, overconfidence, loss aversion repeat across all timescales. A scalp trade and a long-term investment differ only in temporal amplitude, not in emotional architecture. Market structure, therefore, is fractal because human emotion is fractal.

Once a trader perceives this, they cease seeking certainty in data and begin reading rhythm in patterns recognizing that structure emerges not from prediction but from recursive perception.

Practical Exercise: Mapping Cognitive Feedback

Objective: To identify and reprogram self-reinforcing emotional loops that distort probability perception.

1. **Observation Phase:** After each trade, record the dominant emotion (e.g., fear, greed, overconfidence, hesitation).

2. **Reaction Phase:** Document how this emotion influenced your next decision position size, entry timing, or trade avoidance.

3. **Feedback Phase:** Note whether the subsequent outcome reinforced or corrected your emotion.

4. **Pattern Phase:** After several sessions, identify repeating emotional patterns and their market triggers.

Reflection: Ask yourself

> Which emotions amplify clarity and composure? Which amplify distortion? What emotional tone accompanies your best probabilistic decisions?

This mapping transforms unconscious feedback into conscious calibration, allowing emotional energy to serve as a signal rather than interference.

Breaking the Loop: Conscious Interruption

Feedback cannot be eliminated, but it can be reshaped. The key is to create micro-moments of interruption small gaps of awareness that dissolve reactivity before it cascades into distortion.

- When excitement rises, pause and breathe. Revisit your position sizing.

- When fear constricts focus, widen your perspective zoom out one timeframe.
- When revenge or overconfidence appears, step back and reduce exposure.

Each interruption resets the loop, returning perception to neutrality. Over time, these conscious resets rewire cognitive patterns, establishing a new baseline of probabilistic awareness.

Meta-Recursion: Awareness as Feedback

At advanced levels of trading consciousness, feedback itself becomes the object of observation. The trader senses when market rhythm tightens when collective recursion accelerates into mania or despair and notices their internal state mirroring that rhythm.

In this awareness, action becomes non-reactive. The trader neither resists nor indulges emotion but observes it as information. This state *meta-recursive awareness* marks the transition from reactive trading to conscious participation.

> When you can observe your own feedback while perceiving the market's feedback, you are no longer inside the loop you are the awareness that contains it.

This is not detachment, but alignment. Trading becomes an act of synchronized cognition between self and system.

Closing Reflection

Markets are recursive mirrors of human thought and emotion. Every trend, reversal, and volatility cluster reflects cognitive feedback loops unfolding in real time. Mastery lies not in predicting the loops, but in recognizing when you are entangled in them and learning to see both yourself and the market as co-evolving systems of perception.

To trade consciously is to embrace recursion as an ally rather than an enemy. Awareness transforms feedback into insight, emotion into energy, and uncertainty into opportunity. When the trader attains this alignment, they move beyond reaction into resonance a state where the market's rhythm and the mind's rhythm harmonize into one coherent field of probabilistic awareness.

Key Takeaways:

- Markets and minds are recursive systems each influencing and reflecting the other.
- Emotional states form internal feedback loops that shape future perception.

- Recognizing recursive amplification allows traders to anticipate extremes.
- Conscious interruption and journaling help reprogram reactive feedback.
- Awareness transforms feedback into coherence, bridging emotion and probability.

12.2 Aligning Mental Models with Market Rhythms

The Trader's Inner Compass

Markets do not move randomly; they oscillate, pulse, and breathe with collective emotion. Yet, many traders approach them as if they were mechanical systems governed by linear logic. The most consistent traders know that success lies not in fighting uncertainty, but in aligning with it understanding the deeper rhythm beneath price fluctuations.

Every trader operates through a *mental model* an inner map of how they believe markets work. This model filters perception, interprets signals, and guides decisions. However, like any map, it is a simplification of reality. The goal is not to perfect the model, but to continuously evolve it to make it rhythmically congruent with the living market.

When your mental model resonates with the market's natural frequency, decision-making feels fluid and intuitive. When it conflicts, trading becomes a struggle an effort to impose expectation over flow.

The Market as a Living System

Imagine the market as an ocean. Each wave is a collective expression of thousands of decisions fear, greed, anticipation, and relief all merging into one continuous motion. You cannot control the wave, but you can learn to surf it. The trader's task is to sense when the tide is turning, when the undertow is building, and when stillness precedes motion.

In this sense, markets are not mechanical but biological constantly adapting, self-referential, and recursive. Each participant observes others, and their own behavior modifies what they observe. This creates what can be called a *cognitive feedback loop* a dynamic system where thought influences price, and price influences thought.

To align with these rhythms, one must cultivate perceptual flexibility: the ability to update internal beliefs without attachment. This demands awareness of one's own biases confirmation bias, recency bias, and the illusion of control and learning to treat the market not as an opponent, but as a mirror.

The Mirror Principle

The market mirrors the collective consciousness of its participants. But more profoundly, it mirrors you. When you are anxious, you see threat; when you are greedy, you see opportunity where none exists. The act of trading thus becomes a psychological dialogue a dance between inner state and outer signal.

> "The price does not just reflect the crowd it reflects the observer observing the crowd."

The disciplined trader realizes that their emotional state is not noise to suppress, but data to interpret. Fear can be a signal of excessive position size; euphoria can mark the peak of complacency. Aligning your mental model requires using emotional information as part of your analytical process, not separate from it.

Rhythms, Cycles, and Cognitive Resonance

Every market exhibits multi-layered rhythms: micro-patterns (order flow, intraday liquidity), meso-cycles (weekly sentiment shifts, volatility expansion), and macro trends (monetary policy, credit cycles). The adept trader learns to synchronize with the dominant rhythm without losing awareness of the others.

Cognitive resonance occurs when a trader's mental model is synchronized with the underlying market frequency. At such moments, probability estimation, risk-taking, and intuition align. You are not predicting the future; you are perceiving it as it unfolds.

This state resembles what athletes call *flow* a condition of effortless attention, where action and awareness merge. In trading, flow manifests when your preparation meets the market's tempo: you recognize structure as it forms, respond without hesitation, and risk feels measured rather than forced.

Practical Alignment Exercises

1. The Market Pulse Journal After each trading session, record not only what the market did, but how it *felt*. Note tempo, volatility, and collective behavior. Over time, patterns emerge: you begin to sense when markets are expanding or contracting, when traders are risk-seeking or risk-averse. This develops a kinesthetic sense of rhythm.

2. Cognitive Calibration Before placing a trade, write down your hypothesis, the opposing view, and what data would invalidate your thesis. This simple act reduces cognitive rigidity and keeps your perception adaptive. It reminds you that your model is a working hypothesis, not a truth.

3. Emotional Mapping Each emotion you experience during trading corresponds to a cognitive distortion. Fear may indicate attachment to outcome; anger often reflects violated expectation. By journaling emotional spikes alongside trades, you can recalibrate both position sizing and mindset.

4. Flow Simulation During backtesting, focus less on numerical optimization and more on the *decision rhythm.* Replay market sequences and notice where hesitation or overreaction occurred. Your aim is to internalize the flow of pattern recognition and risk adjustment not to memorize data.

The Paradox of Control

To align with market rhythms is to surrender the illusion of control. The paradox is that mastery emerges only when control is replaced by conscious participation. You cannot force the market to reward you; you can only align with its probabilistic nature.

The market, like music, cannot be dominated it must be felt. If you try to dictate its tempo, you create dissonance; if you listen, you find harmony. Great traders are not predictors of price; they are interpreters of rhythm.

> "You do not predict the next note you listen for where the melody wants to go."

In probabilistic domains, such as trading, this form of alignment yields what could be called *dynamic intuition*: a fusion of statistical reasoning, emotional awareness, and embodied pattern recognition.

Integration: From Belief to Flow

The evolution of a trader's mind is a recursive process each feedback loop between perception and outcome refines the mental model. This recursive refinement transforms trading from a reactive act into a creative practice.

When perception aligns with probability, and probability aligns with rhythm, you no longer trade against the market you trade within it. You become part of its pulse.

Reflect on your last ten trades. For each trade, consider:

1. How closely did my perception match the actual market rhythm?
2. Did I project my expectations, or did I adapt to the evolving market structure?
3. What feedback did the market offer about the accuracy of my belief model?

After reviewing all trades, summarize your key insights and adjust one specific aspect of your trading process to improve market alignment.

Closing Reflection

Markets reward not prediction, but coherence between mind, model, and motion. The journey of an advanced trader is thus not toward certainty, but toward rhythmic awareness. You learn to feel probability, to trust the interplay between logic and intuition, and to act with deliberate humility.

Alignment is not static; it is a continuous recalibration between thought and flow. The more flexible your model, the closer you come to harmony with the market's music the subtle pulse beneath chaos.

> "In the end, the market is not to be conquered it is to be understood, and through understanding, to be danced with."

12.3 Feedback Loop Exercises

Introduction

Understanding feedback loops in trading is not merely an academic pursuit it is the practical key to synchronizing perception, action, and outcome. Markets are inherently recursive: every action by a trader influences price, which in turn modifies future actions of oneself and others. Recognizing these loops transforms reactive trading into conscious, adaptive engagement.

In this section, we explore exercises designed to make feedback loops tangible, actionable, and personally insightful. These exercises cultivate awareness of the cyclical nature of markets, sharpen probabilistic thinking, and train traders to respond adaptively rather than impulsively.

Exercise 1: Mapping Cognitive Loops

1. Select a recent series of trades or market observations.
2. Draw a diagram linking your perception, decisions, market reactions, and emotional responses.
3. Identify points where your interpretation fed back into your action, amplifying or dampening subsequent responses.
4. Reflect: which loops were constructive? Which introduced noise or distortion?

Analogy: Think of this as observing ripples in a pond. Each stone you throw (action) creates concentric ripples (market reactions), which interact with ripples from other stones (other traders' actions) to create complex interference patterns. Your goal is to perceive these interference patterns and anticipate their effects.

Exercise 2: Temporal Feedback Awareness

1. During a trading session, note the lag between market signal and your decision.
2. Track the effect of your action on subsequent price movement over multiple intervals (5–30 minutes).
3. Evaluate whether your decisions accelerated, slowed, or distorted market trends relative to your expectations.
4. Adjust mental timing and decision thresholds accordingly.

Reflection: Often, traders act too quickly, amplifying volatility, or too slowly, missing probabilistic alignment. Feedback awareness trains the mind to integrate the timing of perception with the rhythm of the market.

Exercise 3: Emotional Feedback Loops

1. Identify recurrent emotional triggers in your trading: fear of loss, regret, overconfidence, or excitement.
2. For each trigger, chart the sequence: emotion → perception distortion → decision → market response → emotional reaction.
3. Practice intervening at the perception stage: label the emotion, pause, recalibrate probabilities, then act.
4. Repeat daily for two weeks, gradually shortening the lag between recognition and intervention.

Narrative Insight: One trader reported that by systematically observing emotional feedback, she avoided two impulsive exits during volatile sessions, preserving both capital and confidence. The feedback loop, once conscious, became a source of clarity rather than chaos.

Exercise 4: Probabilistic Feedback Simulation

1. Create hypothetical trades with assigned subjective probabilities.
2. Simulate market reactions using historical volatility or random noise.
3. Record outcomes, analyze divergence between expectation and actual market behavior.
4. Reflect: where did your model correctly anticipate feedback? Where did it fail? Adjust your mental model iteratively.

Analogy: This is akin to tuning a musical instrument in varying acoustic environments. The goal is not to achieve absolute perfection, but to calibrate your expectations to the environment's natural variability.

Exercise 5: Recursive Journaling

1. Maintain a journal capturing three layers: action, market response, and self-reflection.
2. Note any recurring patterns: for example, "After entering long positions during intraday spikes, I tend to overestimate continuation probability."
3. Update your trading rules or mental heuristics based on this feedback.
4. Over time, your journal becomes a living model of adaptive feedback loops.

Philosophical Reflection

Feedback loops reveal the market as a co-created reality: traders shape the market as much as it shapes them. Every decision, every reaction, is both input and output in a probabilistic, dynamic system. Recognizing this duality fosters humility and strategic insight.

As in life, it is not the absence of disturbance that leads to mastery, but the capacity to perceive, adapt, and act coherently amidst it. Feedback loops transform from potential traps into instruments of learning and alignment.

Closing Thoughts

Mastery of feedback loops is mastery of self within the market. By mapping cognitive loops, observing temporal effects, managing emotional interference, simulating probabilistic outcomes, and recursive journaling, traders develop adaptive intelligence.

This intelligence allows traders to transform market complexity into actionable insight, aligning perception, probability, and action in a continuous, conscious cycle. In the probabilistic world of financial markets, feedback loop exercises are not optional they are essential for sustained performance, emotional resilience, and strategic advantage.

Chapter 13

Entangled Decision Networks

Financial markets are not isolated mechanisms; they are intricate webs of interdependent decisions. Each trader, algorithm, and institution participates in a vast network where choices reverberate across time and space. Understanding this entanglement is essential for advanced traders who aim to anticipate, rather than merely react to, market dynamics.

In this chapter, we explore the concept of *Entangled Decision Networks* how individual and collective behaviors create correlated movements across assets, sectors, and geographies. We examine methods to recognize patterns emerging from these networks, understand the underlying market correlations, and identify moments when synchronization across traders or instruments can signal opportunities or risks.

Through conceptual insights, narrative examples, and practical exercises, this chapter equips traders to see markets as dynamic, interconnected decision systems. By aligning perception and analysis with the emergent structure of these networks, traders can enhance both probabilistic reasoning and strategic foresight.

13.1 Recognizing Collective Behavioral Patterns

In the vast, interconnected ecosystem of financial markets, individual decisions rarely exist in isolation. Each participant whether a retail trader, institutional investor, or algorithm interacts within a network of perceptions, expectations, and actions. The aggregation of these actions gives rise to collective behavioral patterns, emergent phenomena that are probabilistic in nature and often reveal more than the sum of their parts.

Conceptual Overview

Collective behavioral patterns emerge when the aggregated actions of market participants synchronize into identifiable structures. These can manifest as:

- Herding behavior, where traders converge on similar trades.
- Volatility clustering, where price fluctuations group in time.
- Cross-asset correlations, where multiple securities move in tandem due to shared macroeconomic drivers or sentiment.

These patterns are not deterministic they do not guarantee outcomes but they illuminate probabilistic tendencies. Recognizing them requires a shift from viewing the market as a collection of isolated signals to perceiving it as a living, adaptive network.

Analogy: The Murmuration

Consider a murmuration of starlings at twilight. Each bird follows simple rules: maintain a minimal distance from neighbors, align with their flight path, and avoid collisions. Yet, the collective exhibits fluid, synchronized patterns that cannot be predicted by observing a single bird. Markets behave in a similar fashion: individual decisions are simple, yet their interactions generate complex, emergent structures. Traders attuned to these patterns can anticipate waves of sentiment, momentum shifts, and volatility clustering.

Narrative Insight

Imagine a sudden surge in technology stocks across multiple exchanges. A trader examining only a single stock might see randomness. However, a perceptive trader recognizes correlated movements, driven by algorithmic activity, macroeconomic indicators, and collective investor psychology. By understanding these collective patterns, the trader can adjust positions, manage risk, and align with the emergent probability cloud rather than reacting impulsively.

Practical Exercise 1: Mapping Collective Patterns

1. Select a set of correlated assets (stocks, commodities, or currencies).
2. Track their intraday and daily movements, noting synchronized trends or reversals.
3. Document clusters of coordinated behavior along with contextual triggers such as news events, sentiment shifts, or trading volume spikes.
4. Assign probabilistic expectations for pattern recurrence in future sessions.

5. Refine your mental model by comparing predicted outcomes with actual behavior, iterating continuously.

Practical Exercise 2: Detecting Emotional Herding

1. Monitor real-time sentiment analytics, social media discussions, or news feeds during volatile market periods.

2. Observe correlations between sentiment shifts and asset price movements.

3. Identify episodes where collective emotion fear, greed, or euphoria drives coordinated trading behavior.

4. Adjust exposure or position sizing according to probabilistic alignment with collective dynamics.

Reflective Practice

Advanced traders cultivate meta-awareness of their role within the collective. Regularly ask: *Am I reacting to emergent market patterns, or am I observing them objectively?* Maintain a journal that captures trades, emotional responses, and probabilistic expectations. Over time, this reflective practice strengthens anticipatory insight, transforming reactive behavior into conscious decision-making.

Philosophical Perspective

Markets are mirrors of collective cognition. Recognizing behavioral patterns allows traders to convert apparent randomness into structured information. By observing and decoding these patterns, one aligns perception with probabilistic realities, creating a coherence between thought, emotion, and action. In this sense, the perceptive trader acts as both an observer and a participant, harmonizing individual decisions with the emergent rhythm of the market.

13.2 Decision Networks and Market Correlations

Financial markets operate not as isolated instruments but as interconnected networks of decisions. Each trader's action whether a market order, limit placement, or algorithmic signal propagates through the network, influencing others in subtle and sometimes dramatic ways. Understanding these decision networks and their correlations is essential for discerning market structure, anticipating emergent behavior, and navigating probabilistic dynamics.

Conceptual Overview

Decision networks consist of nodes (traders, institutions, algorithms) and links (information flows, behavioral influence, capital allocation). Market correlations arise when the decisions of nodes are interdependent, leading to observable synchronization across assets, sectors, or entire markets. These correlations can be:

- Structural: resulting from macroeconomic factors, policy changes, or regulatory frameworks.
- Behavioral: driven by shared sentiment, herding, or emotional contagion.
- Algorithmic: induced by automated strategies reacting to overlapping signals.

Recognizing these networks requires viewing markets as dynamic systems where each decision contributes probabilistically to the next, creating emergent correlations and feedback loops.

Analogy: Neural Networks and Market Cognition

Imagine a neural network in the brain. Each neuron fires based on inputs from connected neurons, and patterns of firing produce cognition, perception, and action. Similarly, traders are like neurons in a global decision network. Signals propagate, reactions amplify, and collective behavior emerges. Patterns observed in one segment of the market can cascade, creating correlations that reflect the interconnected cognition of participants.

Narrative Insight

Consider the 2008 financial crisis. Mortgage-backed securities and derivatives were deeply correlated due to overlapping risk exposures and decision networks spanning banks, rating agencies, and institutional investors. Individual actions, taken in isolation, seemed rational. Yet, the network effects created systemic risk, magnifying outcomes far beyond individual intent. Traders aware of network dynamics anticipate such correlations, assessing not just isolated probabilities but systemic interactions.

Practical Exercise 1: Mapping Decision Networks

1. Select a cluster of related assets (e.g., tech stocks, commodities, or currency pairs).
2. Track market activity, noting simultaneous movements, volume spikes, and cross-asset correlations.

3. Document the sequence of observed decisions, identifying which actors (institutions, funds, retail traders, algorithms) may have influenced others.

4. Visualize the network, mapping nodes and links to understand pathways of influence and emergent patterns.

5. Reflect on how your trading strategy can align with or counter these network dynamics.

Practical Exercise 2: Correlation Stress Testing

1. Define scenarios where correlated assets may decouple or exaggerate trends.

2. Assign probabilistic weights to each scenario based on historical behavior and market sentiment.

3. Simulate decision propagation through your portfolio, adjusting exposure and hedges according to network-induced probabilities.

4. Analyze outcomes and refine your mental models to anticipate cascading effects in real-time.

Reflective Practice

Advanced traders cultivate an awareness of their position within the network. Periodically, ask: *Which decisions am I amplifying or dampening? How do my actions ripple through the market network?* Journaling these reflections enhances meta-cognition, allowing for deliberate alignment with probabilistic structures rather than reactive participation.

Philosophical Perspective

Markets are more than price charts they are living networks of interdependent decisions. By observing correlations and tracing decision pathways, traders decode collective cognition, gaining insight into the hidden forces shaping probabilities. In doing so, they not only perceive market patterns but also consciously position themselves within the network, harmonizing strategy, perception, and probabilistic awareness. Awareness of decision networks transforms trading from a solitary endeavor into a dialogue with the collective intelligence of the market.

13.3 Reading Synchronization Across Assets

Markets are rarely composed of isolated instruments; they exist as interconnected systems where assets often move in coordinated patterns. Recognizing synchronization across assets whether through correlations, leading-lagging relationships, or sentiment propagation allows traders to anticipate probabilistic trends and align their decisions with the collective rhythm of the market.

Conceptual Overview

Synchronization emerges when multiple assets respond to shared information, macroeconomic signals, or correlated behavioral patterns among market participants. These connections are probabilistic rather than deterministic: a movement in one asset does not guarantee movement in another, but it changes the likelihood and timing of related outcomes.

- **Direct Correlation:** Assets that respond similarly to a common driver, such as commodities affected by interest rates or energy prices linked to geopolitical events.
- **Inverse Correlation:** Assets that move in opposite directions due to hedging strategies or portfolio balancing.
- **Lagged Synchronization:** Sequential responses where one asset leads and another follows, often revealing hidden causal structures or behavioral feedback loops.

Analogy: The Orchestra of Markets

Consider an orchestra performing a symphony. Each instrument contributes independently, yet the ensemble produces coherent harmony. A sudden accent in the percussion may subtly shift the interpretation of the strings, creating a ripple effect. Similarly, traders who perceive synchronization across assets sense the underlying "music" of market probabilities, responding in harmony rather than in dissonance.

Narrative Insight

Imagine a trader monitoring equities, bonds, and commodities. She notices that when bond yields spike, technology stocks begin to decline, followed by correlated movement in commodity futures. By mapping these sequential patterns and their probabilities, she anticipates market shifts before conventional indicators signal action. Synchronization is not merely correlation it is the perception of interwoven probabilities and behavioral alignment across assets.

Practical Exercise 1: Multi-Asset Correlation Mapping

1. Select a basket of related assets across multiple markets (equities, bonds, commodities, currencies).

2. Track daily or intraday price movements and calculate correlation coefficients or probabilistic associations.
3. Identify periods of high synchronization and note triggers such as news events, macroeconomic releases, or sentiment shifts.
4. Visualize these relationships in a dynamic diagram or heatmap to internalize the network of interactions.

Practical Exercise 2: Leading-Lagging Probability Analysis

1. Identify a candidate "leading" asset whose movements historically precede changes in related instruments.
2. Assign probabilities to potential outcomes in the "lagging" assets based on the leading asset's current behavior.
3. Simulate trades or portfolio adjustments under different probability scenarios, testing decision alignment with observed synchronization.
4. Reflect on discrepancies and update mental models to refine prediction accuracy.

Reflective Practice

Ask yourself: *Which assets are communicating shared probabilities? How does my position resonate with the emergent patterns of the market?* Journaling these insights after trading sessions cultivates meta-awareness, enabling conscious adjustments that account for interconnected risk and opportunity.

Philosophical Perspective

Synchronization across assets illustrates the market as a living network of probabilistic interactions rather than a collection of isolated instruments. Observing and understanding these patterns is akin to perceiving the hidden currents beneath the surface of the ocean waves of collective cognition and sentiment that shape outcomes. Traders who attune to these currents transform from reactive participants into aligned observers and contributors, navigating markets with both intuition and probabilistic precision.

Chapter 14

Coherence vs Decoherence in Trading

In the high-stakes environment of financial markets, the clarity of perception and the alignment of thought directly influence decision quality. Traders experience periods of coherence when cognition, intuition, and emotion are harmonized interspersed with episodes of decoherence, where mental noise, stress, or emotional turbulence distorts probabilistic assessment.

Understanding coherence and decoherence is critical for navigating markets not as a purely mechanical system, but as a complex, perception-dependent landscape. Coherence allows traders to interpret signals accurately, anticipate emergent patterns, and act in alignment with probabilistic expectations. Decoherence, on the other hand, amplifies biases, increases reactionary behavior, and heightens the risk of errors, often when market uncertainty is at its peak.

This chapter explores the mechanisms that sustain mental and emotional coherence, methods to minimize noise-induced decision errors, and practical exercises for cultivating a resilient, focused, and probabilistically aligned mindset. By integrating cognitive science, behavioral finance, and mindfulness-based strategies, traders can train their awareness to maintain equilibrium amid the dynamic flows of the market, transforming mental coherence from a conceptual ideal into a tangible skill.

14.1 Sustaining Emotional and Cognitive Coherence

In trading, coherence refers to the alignment of mind, emotion, and perception a state where intuition, analysis, and probabilistic reasoning operate in harmony. When coherence is present, a trader's decisions reflect both situational awareness and probabilistic insight, creating a flow where perception naturally aligns with market dynamics. When coherence falters, cognitive noise, emotional turbulence, and reactionary impulses distort probability estimates, often resulting in suboptimal or erratic trades.

The Concept of Mental Coherence

Mental coherence can be likened to a finely tuned orchestra. Each instrument emotion, cognition, intuition has its own tone, yet the music emerges from the precise interplay of all components. If one section dominates or falls out of rhythm, the harmony is lost. Similarly, in trading, unchecked fear, greed, or overanalysis can overpower probabilistic reasoning, disrupting the flow of decision-making.

Analogy: Imagine a sailboat navigating a turbulent sea. The market is the ever-changing wind and waves, while the trader's mind is the rigging and sails. Coherence allows the boat to harness external forces efficiently; decoherence leads to capsizing or drifting off course.

Techniques for Sustaining Coherence

1. **Mindful Anchoring:** Regularly check in with both physical and mental states. Focused breathing, posture awareness, or a brief mindfulness pause can restore equilibrium during volatile trading periods.

2. **Cognitive Labeling:** Name the emotions you are experiencing in real time fear, excitement, impatience and note their intensity on a 1–10 scale. Recognizing emotion without judgment reduces reactive impulses.

3. **Pre-Trade Alignment Rituals:** Before initiating a trade, review probabilistic assessments, risk exposure, and emotional readiness. Ask: *Am I perceiving the probabilities clearly, or am I being influenced by residual emotion?* This fosters a deliberate, coherent entry.

4. **Feedback Integration:** Post-trade reflection on both outcomes and decision processes strengthens the coherence loop. Evaluate whether emotional states aligned with probabilistic reasoning, and adjust strategies for future scenarios.

Practical Exercise: Coherence Checkpoints

1. Divide your trading session into intervals (e.g., every 30 minutes).

2. At each interval, pause and assess:

    - Emotional state: dominant emotions and intensity.
    - Cognitive clarity: Are probabilistic judgments consistent with objective data?

- Behavioral alignment: Are actions reflective of calculated risk-reward profiles?

3. Document findings and apply minor adjustments if coherence is slipping.
4. Over time, this exercise strengthens meta-awareness, allowing preemptive correction before significant decoherence occurs.

Narrative Insight

Consider a trader facing a rapid market reversal. Fear rises sharply, tempting a knee-jerk exit. By engaging in mindful anchoring, labeling the emotion as *"intense fear, rated 8/10"*, and reviewing pre-assessed probabilities, the trader stabilizes cognition. Instead of reactionary selling, she adjusts position sizing and hedges exposure, making a decision coherent with market probabilities rather than emotional turbulence. This coherence becomes both a strategic advantage and a method for emotional resilience.

Philosophical Reflection

Coherence is not about suppressing emotion or forcing rationality; it is about harmonizing internal states to resonate with external uncertainty. Emotional and cognitive alignment amplifies perception, enhances probabilistic clarity, and allows the trader to act with intentionality rather than compulsion. In essence, sustaining coherence is the art of being fully present, fully aware, and fully aligned with the market's probabilistic rhythm.

Closing Thoughts

Sustaining emotional and cognitive coherence transforms trading from a reactive, emotionally driven endeavor into a conscious, probabilistically informed practice. Through mindful anchoring, cognitive labeling, pre-trade alignment, and iterative feedback, traders cultivate resilience, clarity, and adaptive insight. Mastery of coherence is mastery over the human component of markets, turning mental alignment into strategic advantage and the unpredictable tides of trading into a field for conscious, intentional action.

14.2 Avoiding Noise-Induced Decision Errors

Financial markets are inherently noisy systems, saturated with a constant flow of information: breaking news, price fluctuations, analyst opinions, social media sentiment, and economic data releases. This ambient noise can easily distort perception, inflate reactionary impulses, and misalign probabilistic reasoning. Advanced traders recognize that the challenge is not merely analyzing data but distinguishing signal from noise, and ensuring that decisions reflect underlying probabilities rather than ephemeral distractions.

The Nature of Market Noise

Market noise is analogous to static on a radio frequency. While the signal true probabilistic information is present, it is often masked by interference. Traders who respond to every fluctuation, rumor, or headline risk amplifying small perturbations into outsized decisions. Over time, this creates behavioral fatigue, erodes consistency, and increases cognitive decoherence.

Analogy: Imagine sailing a small boat in turbulent waters. If the sailor reacts to every ripple and gust, the vessel may overcorrect, losing stability and direction. A skilled sailor, however, discerns the patterns of prevailing currents and adjusts only for meaningful deviations. Similarly, traders must filter out minor market fluctuations and focus on the structural forces shaping probabilities.

Cognitive Mechanisms Behind Noise-Induced Errors

- **Recency Bias:** Overweighting recent events or price movements, causing disproportionate reactions.
- **Availability Heuristic:** Making judgments based on information that is most accessible or sensational, rather than probabilistically relevant.
- **Overtrading Impulses:** Responding to every noise signal with new positions or hedges, disrupting portfolio coherence.
- **Emotional Amplification:** Fear or greed magnifies the perceived importance of transient information, distorting objective risk-reward assessments.

Practical Framework for Filtering Noise

1. **Define Probabilistic Criteria:** Establish explicit thresholds for action based on expected value, probability-weighted outcomes, and risk tolerances. Any market movement or news item not meeting these thresholds is treated as background noise.
2. **Implement Temporal Buffering:** Introduce short delays before reacting to new information. For instance, instead of immediately executing trades after a news release, pause to observe initial market reactions and evaluate whether they meaningfully alter the probabilistic landscape.
3. **Signal-to-Noise Journaling:** Maintain a log of market events, trades, and decisions, distinguishing between high-probability signals and transient noise. Over time, patterns emerge that refine judgment and enhance probabilistic clarity.

4. **Mindfulness Anchoring:** Use brief mindfulness techniques to recognize emotional spikes triggered by market chatter. Label emotions ("excitement," "fear," "urgency"), observe without judgment, and allow rational probability assessments to dominate decision-making.

Exercise: Noise-Filtering Simulation

1. Collect a list of recent market headlines or price fluctuations over a fixed period.

2. Evaluate each item against pre-defined probabilistic thresholds:

    - Does this event significantly shift expected outcomes?
    - Is there sufficient data to quantify impact?
    - Does acting now improve expected value, or merely react to transient noise?

3. Rank items as *signal*, *background noise*, or *irrelevant*.

4. Reflect on decisions made in real-time versus those informed by deliberate filtering. Adjust future criteria accordingly.

Narrative Insight

A professional trader recounted facing a sudden flurry of contradictory news: a major economic report, social media speculation, and a high-profile investor's tweet. Initially, her impulses urged rapid adjustment of positions. By engaging her noise-filtering framework evaluating probabilistic impact, waiting 15 minutes to observe market reaction, and journaling emotional responses she avoided overtrading and aligned her decisions with true probabilistic signals. The result was both a measurable performance advantage and emotional equilibrium.

Philosophical Reflection

Noise is not inherently negative; it is the medium in which true market probabilities exist. Attempting to eliminate noise entirely is futile. The trader's mastery lies in discerning which elements merit attention and which are ephemeral distractions. By cultivating awareness, applying probabilistic filters, and integrating reflective exercises, one transforms noise from a source of error into a contextual backdrop against which clarity and coherence emerge.

Closing Thoughts

Avoiding noise-induced decision errors is a skill that integrates perception, probability, and conscious awareness. Through deliberate frameworks, journaling, mindfulness, and probabilistic thresholds, traders maintain coherence, protect capital, and enhance decision quality. In the chaotic flow of modern markets, this disciplined approach allows one to act with intention, not compulsion, converting environmental turbulence into a field for informed, adaptive trading.

14.3 Training for Mental Coherence

Mental coherence is the alignment of cognition, emotion, and perception in service of probabilistic decision-making. In high-stakes trading, coherence is not a passive state but an actively cultivated skill. It enables traders to perceive market probabilities accurately, integrate multiple streams of information without fragmentation, and act decisively without being hijacked by emotional turbulence or cognitive bias.

The Philosophy of Mental Coherence

Coherence is akin to the harmonic resonance of an orchestra: each instrument (thought, emotion, perception) contributes to a unified, expressive whole. Discordant notes unmanaged fear, overconfidence, or fragmented attention produce cognitive noise, distorting decision-making. By training coherence, the trader tunes these elements into a synergistic system, capable of perceiving probabilistic patterns and responding adaptively.

Analogy: Consider a tightrope walker navigating a thin wire in strong wind. Success is not guaranteed by balance alone; it requires anticipatory adjustments, calm focus, and integrated sensory feedback. Similarly, a coherent mind perceives market currents, anticipates probabilistic shifts, and adjusts trading strategies with minimal internal friction.

Core Practices for Cultivating Mental Coherence

1. **Structured Mindfulness:** Begin each trading session with a brief mindfulness routine. Focus on breath, bodily sensations, and present-moment awareness to stabilize attention. This practice reduces reactive impulses and cultivates clarity under uncertainty.

2. **Cognitive Integration Exercises:** Periodically challenge yourself to integrate multiple market indicators and scenarios without jumping to immediate conclusions. For example, mentally simulate three competing outcomes for a given asset, noting how each probability interacts with portfolio exposure.

3. **Emotional Anchoring:** Identify reliable techniques deep breathing, visualization, or brief pauses to regulate heightened emotional states. Apply anchors when detecting fear, excitement, or frustration, ensuring emotions enhance rather than distort probabilistic reasoning.

4. **Meta-Cognitive Reflection:** Maintain a trading journal not only for outcomes but also for mental and emotional states. Reflect on moments of clarity, indecision, or emotional hijack. Over time, patterns emerge, enabling proactive adjustments for coherence.

5. **Decision Pre-Planning:** Before entering the market, define probabilistic thresholds, risk tolerances, and contingency plans. Pre-planning synchronizes intention with action, reducing cognitive friction and preserving coherence under pressure.

Exercise: Coherence Simulation

1. Select a trading scenario with multiple potential outcomes.

2. Mentally simulate each outcome, including emotional responses and cognitive interpretations.

3. Apply your mindfulness and emotional anchoring techniques to maintain clarity.

4. Decide on the optimal action based on integrated probabilistic assessment.

5. Compare your simulated decision with actual outcomes and reflect on discrepancies to enhance future coherence.

Narrative Insight

A professional trader described a volatile morning in which multiple correlated assets moved unpredictably. Instead of reacting to each micro-movement, he activated his coherence routines: structured breathing, scenario visualization, and journaling of emotional spikes. The result was a calm, decisive set of trades aligned with his probabilistic models. His portfolio remained protected, and his decision-making efficiency improved significantly.

Philosophical Reflection

Coherence is not mere emotional regulation or rational analysis; it is the dynamic interplay of perception, emotion, and probabilistic cognition. Traders often underestimate the degree to which internal fragmentation undermines their decisions. By deliberately cultivating coherence, one achieves a state where mind and market interact harmoniously, allowing probabilistic insight to guide action without interference from reactive impulses.

Closing Thoughts

Training for mental coherence transforms trading from a reactive, stress-laden activity into a conscious, adaptive practice. Through structured mindfulness, cognitive integration, emotional anchoring, meta-cognitive reflection, and pre-planned decision protocols, traders cultivate resilience, clarity, and precision. In probabilistic markets, where uncertainty is constant, mental coherence becomes both a competitive advantage and a foundation for sustainable performance, enabling the trader to perceive, decide, and act in harmonious alignment with market probabilities.

Chapter 15

The Quantum Decision-Making Framework

In the probabilistic landscape of financial markets, decision-making transcends simple analysis of price charts or historical patterns. It is a dynamic interplay between observation, probability assessment, emotional calibration, and conscious action. The Quantum Decision-Making Framework offers a structured approach to navigate uncertainty with clarity, precision, and adaptive flexibility.

At its core, the framework emphasizes four interdependent phases: **Observe**, **Probabilize**, **Align**, and **Act**. Each phase represents a conscious engagement with both internal and external factors, harmonizing perception, cognition, and action. By iteratively cycling through these phases, traders cultivate a resilient decision-making process that adapts to shifting market probabilities and emotional states.

This framework is not static. It encourages reflection, iterative learning, and continuous refinement, allowing traders to internalize probabilistic reasoning, integrate behavioral insights, and synchronize their cognitive and emotional systems with market dynamics. Throughout this chapter, we explore each phase in depth, illustrate practical applications, and provide exercises to foster mastery of this integrative approach.

The Quantum Decision-Making Framework is designed for advanced traders seeking more than tactical execution. It is a philosophy of trading as a conscious practice a way to perceive probabilities, harness emotional intelligence, and act decisively in alignment with the rhythms of the market.

15.1 Observe → Probabilize → Align → Act

Financial markets are not deterministic machines; they are living systems shaped by human behavior, collective cognition, and probabilistic dynamics. To navigate them effectively, traders must move beyond reactive impulses and adopt a structured approach that integrates observation, probability assessment, alignment of mind and emotion, and deliberate action. The **Observe → Probabilize → Align → Act** framework offers precisely this pathway.

1. Observe: Cultivating Awareness

Observation is the foundation of all conscious trading. It is not merely scanning charts or reading news; it is the deliberate act of perceiving the market in its full probabilistic complexity. Observation requires mindfulness an acute awareness of both external price dynamics and internal cognitive and emotional states.

Practical Insight: Consider a trader monitoring a volatile stock. Beyond noting price levels, they observe trading volume spikes, sentiment shifts in social media, and the subtle cues of liquidity changes. Simultaneously, they observe their own mental state: is fear rising? Are biases coloring perception?

Exercise: Maintain a dual observation journal. For every trade setup, record:

1. Market conditions and indicators.
2. Emotional and cognitive states.
3. Any assumptions or biases detected.

This habit sharpens perceptual clarity and reduces the likelihood of subconscious distortions influencing decisions.

2. Probabilize: Quantifying Uncertainty

Once observation is established, the next step is to probabilize to consciously estimate the likelihood of potential outcomes. Markets are inherently uncertain; embracing probabilities allows traders to move from deterministic thinking to a spectrum-based mindset.

Conceptual Insight: Probabilizing is akin to holding multiple market futures simultaneously in your mind, recognizing that each scenario has a weighted chance of materializing. Unlike binary thinking "it will go up or down" probabilizing encourages nuanced expectation and prepares the trader for contingencies.

Exercise: For each trade setup, assign subjective probabilities to at least three scenarios:

1. Bullish outcome
2. Neutral or sideways outcome
3. Bearish outcome

Compare subjective probabilities with objective signals. Over time, this hones intuition and sharpens decision quality.

3. Align: Synchronizing Mind, Emotion, and Market Probabilities

Alignment bridges perception and action. After observing and probabilizing, the trader must synchronize internal states with external probabilistic realities. Emotional regulation, cognitive coherence, and focus are crucial in this phase.

Analogy: Imagine a violinist preparing for a performance. Observing the sheet music (market), understanding harmonic probabilities (potential price outcomes), and tuning the instrument (aligning mind and emotion) all precede the act of playing (trading).

Exercise: Develop a brief pre-trade alignment ritual:

1. Close your eyes and mentally rehearse the trade.
2. Check for emotional intensity: fear, greed, or overconfidence.
3. Breathe deeply and consciously visualize probabilistic scenarios.
4. Adjust position size or exposure to match your probabilistic assessment.

Alignment ensures that decisions are coherent, deliberate, and resilient to reactive impulses.

4. Act: Deliberate, Probability-Aligned Execution

Action is the culmination of observation, probabilization, and alignment. Here, the trader executes with precision, informed by both objective probabilities and calibrated internal states. Importantly, acting in this framework is not impulsive; it is a conscious, iterative engagement with uncertainty.

Practical Insight: When placing an order, consider:

1. Does this action reflect the weighted probabilities you assigned?
2. Are emotional biases minimized?
3. Are contingency plans in place for alternate scenarios?

Exercise: After execution, review outcomes relative to assigned probabilities:

1. Which scenario unfolded?

2. Were your probabilities realistic?
3. How well did alignment translate into action?

This reflective process converts experience into refined probabilistic intuition.

Iterative Nature of the Framework

Observe → Probabilize → Align → Act is not linear. It is iterative and recursive: after action, observation resumes, probabilities are updated, alignment is re-evaluated, and subsequent actions are informed. Over time, this cycle fosters adaptive mastery, enhancing resilience, clarity, and strategic insight.

Narrative Insight

One trader described the framework as the difference between "riding waves" and "being tossed by them." By consciously observing the market, estimating probabilities, aligning mind and emotions, and acting deliberately, uncertainty transforms from a source of fear into a source of opportunity.

Conclusion: This framework integrates perception, probability, emotional calibration, and deliberate action into a cohesive methodology. Advanced traders who internalize this cycle develop an adaptive edge, capable of navigating probabilistic markets with clarity, resilience, and conscious intentionality.

15.2 Adaptive, Iterative Decision Processes

Markets are living, dynamic systems, shaped by the interplay of countless participants, unpredictable events, and feedback loops. Unlike static systems, where inputs lead to predictable outputs, financial markets are inherently probabilistic and non-linear. To navigate this complexity, traders must adopt an **adaptive, iterative approach** one that continuously observes, learns, recalibrates, and executes.

The Philosophy of Iterative Trading

Iteration is more than a technique; it is a mindset. Just as scientists test hypotheses, analyze outcomes, and refine their understanding, traders must treat each decision as an experiment. Markets reveal patterns only through repeated cycles of action and reflection. By iteratively updating mental models, probabilistic estimates, and strategies, traders remain aligned with evolving market dynamics rather than relying on static assumptions.

Analogy: Imagine a musician improvising jazz. Each note depends on what was played before, what is being played now, and what could be played next. Success emerges not from a rigid score but from a responsive, adaptive flow. Similarly, a trader must continuously adjust to the market's "improvisational score," sensing shifts, recalibrating probabilities, and modulating actions accordingly.

Key Components of an Iterative Decision Cycle

1. **Observation:** Carefully monitor price movements, volume, volatility, and market sentiment. Recognize anomalies and emergent patterns. Observation is not passive; it requires mindful awareness of both external market signals and internal cognitive-emotional responses.

2. **Probabilization:** Translate observations into updated probabilistic assessments. For each potential outcome, ask: How likely is this scenario based on current information? This process acknowledges uncertainty and avoids overconfidence in deterministic thinking.

3. **Alignment:** Synchronize perception, cognition, and emotion. Emotional states fear, greed, or hope can distort probability assessments. Iterative alignment ensures decisions reflect objective probabilistic thinking while maintaining mental clarity.

4. **Action:** Execute trades or adjustments based on the aligned probabilities and calibrated mental state. Flexibility is essential decisions must be dynamic, reflecting the latest observations and recalibrations.

5. **Reflection and Feedback:** After each action, analyze outcomes relative to prior probability assessments. Document successes, errors, and emotional reactions. Reflection generates learning, informs future iterations, and gradually refines intuition.

Practical Strategies for Adaptive Iteration

- **Dynamic Probabilistic Models:** Maintain real-time probability estimates for key scenarios and update continuously as new information arrives.

- **Scenario-Based Simulation:** Mentally rehearse multiple market scenarios, including extremes. Pre-plan responses for each potential outcome to reduce reactionary errors.

- **Adaptive Position Sizing:** Adjust exposure according to evolving probabilities and confidence levels. Smaller positions reduce risk during uncertainty; larger positions capitalize on high-probability setups.

- **Reflective Journaling:** Record each trading session, including market conditions, probabilistic assessments, emotional states, and decisions taken. Over time, this builds meta-awareness, allowing pattern recognition and proactive adjustment.

Narrative Insight

One experienced trader described iterative adaptation as "riding a river, not damming it." Instead of forcing the market to conform to pre-conceived rules, he observed currents, adjusted paddling, and flowed with the water's natural motion. By iterating through observation, assessment, alignment, and action, he transformed uncertainty into a strategic advantage, making decisions that were both rational and emotionally coherent.

Philosophical Reflection

Adaptive iteration embraces the impermanence and uncertainty inherent in markets. Attempting to impose rigid control is futile; flexibility, observation, and recalibration are the true sources of mastery. By internalizing iterative processes, traders align themselves with the market's probabilistic nature, transforming uncertainty into a resource rather than an obstacle.

Closing Thoughts

Adaptive, iterative decision processes empower traders to operate with clarity and resilience. By continuously observing, probabilizing, aligning, acting, and reflecting, traders cultivate both technical competence and psychological robustness. In probabilistic markets, iterative adaptation is not optional it is essential for achieving sustained performance, strategic fluidity, and conscious, deliberate trading mastery.

15.3 Reflective Mastery Practices

Mastery in trading is not merely the accumulation of technical knowledge or probabilistic models it is the cultivation of reflective consciousness. Reflective mastery practices allow traders to observe their own mental and emotional processes, learn from experience, and integrate insights into actionable decision-making frameworks. This section explores how deliberate reflection transforms probabilistic reasoning into adaptive wisdom.

The Philosophy of Reflection

Reflection is the bridge between experience and learning. Without reflection, even repeated exposure to market dynamics yields only superficial understanding. Reflective mastery entails analyzing decisions not merely by outcomes, but by the quality of observation, alignment with probabilities, and coherence of emotional and cognitive states. It is the practice of becoming the *observer of one's own decision-making processes*, recognizing patterns, biases, and internal states that shape market perception.

Analogy: Consider a seasoned chess player reviewing a past game. The player does not only note which moves led to victory or defeat; they examine their strategic reasoning, miscalculations, and moments of overconfidence or hesitation. Similarly, a trader reflecting on each market session gains insight into both strategy and self.

Core Practices for Reflective Mastery

1. **Structured Journaling:** Maintain a detailed journal capturing:

    - Market conditions and probabilistic assessments
    - Emotional and cognitive states during key decisions
    - Actions taken and rationale
    - Outcomes relative to expectations

    Over time, this record illuminates recurring behavioral patterns, interference points, and adaptive strengths.

2. **Post-Session Analysis:** After each trading session, allocate time for reflection. Identify moments where perception aligned or misaligned with probability, where emotions interfered, and where iterative adjustments succeeded or failed.

3. **Scenario Decomposition:** Break down critical market scenarios into decision nodes. For each node:

    - Ask what probabilities were considered
    - Examine the influence of emotional or cognitive bias
    - Evaluate alternative choices and outcomes

    This exercise strengthens the ability to anticipate probabilistic outcomes and refine strategy for future iterations.

4. **Meta-Awareness Practices:** Engage in mindfulness or contemplative exercises focused on observing thoughts and emotions as they arise. Recognize the difference between intuitive probabilistic assessments and emotional reactions. Strengthen the ability to pause, reflect, and recalibrate before action.

5. **Reflective Peer Review:** Occasionally discuss trading decisions and reasoning with trusted peers or mentors. External perspectives can reveal blind spots and reinforce disciplined reflection.

Integrating Reflection into Iterative Processes

Reflective mastery is not separate from action it is interwoven into the iterative decision cycle. After each trade or market observation:

1. Observe outcomes relative to initial probabilistic estimates.

2. Analyze discrepancies, identifying whether they arose from informational gaps, emotional interference, or misalignment of mental models.
3. Adjust future probability assignments, decision rules, and emotional calibration strategies.

By embedding reflection into each iteration, the trader continuously evolves, transforming experience into adaptive intelligence.

Exercises for Reflective Mastery

1. **Probability-Emotion Reflection:** For each trade, note how emotions influenced your probability assessment. Reflect on patterns across sessions and adjust calibration strategies.
2. **Outcome vs Expectation Mapping:** Create a visual map comparing expected outcomes with actual results. Annotate deviations with cognitive and emotional observations.
3. **Scenario Replay Journaling:** Mentally replay critical market scenarios and imagine alternative decisions. Reflect on how different alignment of perception, probability, and emotion could have changed the outcome.
4. **Weekly Meta-Review:** Review a week's worth of trades, journaling insights on personal tendencies, emotional patterns, and probabilistic misjudgments. Identify actionable steps for iterative improvement.

Narrative Insight

An advanced trader described reflective mastery as "learning to see the market and yourself simultaneously." During a volatile week, he noticed a subtle pattern of fear-driven early exits. Through journaling and scenario analysis, he traced the source to overreaction to short-term volatility rather than a flaw in probabilistic assessment. By consciously adjusting his emotional response and observing its effects in real-time, he converted a behavioral vulnerability into a source of disciplined insight.

Philosophical Reflection

Reflection illuminates the intersection of mind and market. Markets are probabilistic mirrors, but the clarity of that reflection depends on the observer's awareness. Reflective mastery transforms repetition into wisdom, aligning internal perception with external probabilities and integrating emotion, cognition, and action into a coherent framework.

Closing Thoughts

Reflective mastery practices are the keystone of conscious, adaptive trading. By systematically observing, journaling, analyzing, and integrating lessons, traders develop meta-awareness, refine probabilistic judgment, and enhance emotional and cognitive coherence. In an uncertain, probabilistic market, reflective mastery is the compass that guides the trader from reaction to intentional, resilient, and insightful action.

Part IV

Mastery and Integration

Chapter 16

Synchronizing Mind, Market, & Probability

In the complex landscape of financial markets, mastery arises not only from understanding price movements or probabilities but from the coherent alignment of mind, market, and probabilistic awareness. This chapter explores the art and science of achieving a state where perception, intuition, and action resonate harmoniously with market dynamics.

Markets are probabilistic, fluid, and often nonlinear. A trader's cognitive and emotional states act as lenses through which these dynamics are interpreted. Misalignment between mind and market can lead to reactionary decisions, emotional interference, and probabilistic misjudgments. Conversely, synchronized awareness enables the trader to perceive patterns, anticipate possibilities, and act with clarity and composure.

16.1 Achieving Flow in Probabilistic Markets

Introduction

Flow is the state where perception, cognition, and action align seamlessly, allowing traders to navigate probabilistic markets with clarity and adaptability. Unlike mechanical rule-following, flow is a conscious immersion into the dynamics of uncertainty, where the mind perceives probabilities intuitively and responds with calm, deliberate action.

Markets are inherently probabilistic, driven by countless interacting variables and human behaviors. Attempting to impose deterministic frameworks on such systems often results in reactive, emotionally-driven decisions. Flow represents a higher-order alignment a state in which the trader's consciousness resonates with the market's probabilistic rhythms.

The Nature of Flow in Trading

- **Heightened Awareness:** The trader perceives market cues without distortion, integrating real-time information with probabilistic mental models.
- **Adaptive Responsiveness:** Decisions emerge from the present state rather than from rigid rules or past biases.
- **Temporal Flexibility:** Subjective time stretches or contracts, allowing faster recognition of emerging patterns and slower, reflective analysis where needed.
- **Integrated Emotional-Cognitive State:** Emotional interference is minimized; fear, greed, and hope are observed, acknowledged, and harnessed constructively.
- **Intrinsic Motivation:** Engagement is fueled by curiosity and mastery rather than external rewards.

Why Flow Matters in Probabilistic Markets

Trading is not about predicting certainty it is about navigating uncertainty intelligently. Markets do not respond to intentions; they respond to collective human behavior filtered through probability. Flow allows a trader to:

- Observe complex patterns without distortion.
- Detect subtle probability shifts and divergences in real time.
- Make decisions that are coherent with both internal cognitive states and external market dynamics.
- Maintain composure during extreme volatility.

Analogies for Understanding Flow

1. The Jazz Ensemble Analogy: Just as a jazz musician improvises based on both structure and the ongoing dynamics of the ensemble, a trader in flow adapts to market rhythms without rigidly following preset rules. Awareness, intuition, and probabilistic understanding combine to create adaptive, real-time responses.

2. The Surfing Analogy: Waves represent market possibilities. A surfer does not fight the wave but aligns with its energy, adjusting posture and timing to ride it efficiently. Similarly, a trader in flow synchronizes with probability waves, responding optimally to market currents.

Practical Exercises for Cultivating Flow

Exercise 1: Mindful Observation Drill

1. Begin each session with five minutes of focused breathing or meditation.
2. Identify key probabilistic signals or patterns to observe.
3. Track these without trading, simply noting shifts and emerging possibilities.

Exercise 2: Adaptive Probability Mapping

1. Choose three potential trade setups.
2. Assign subjective probabilities to each outcome.
3. Observe how emotions shift perceived probabilities and recalibrate as needed.

Exercise 3: Real-Time Flow Entry

1. After observation drills, select a trade opportunity aligned with your probability model.
2. Enter trade mindfully, continuously observing emotional and cognitive states.
3. Use breathing, mental anchors, or micro-pauses to maintain clarity.

Exercise 4: Reflective Journaling

1. Document sessions, noting moments of flow and distraction.
2. Analyze triggers that disrupt flow and methods that restore alignment.
3. Review periodically to internalize patterns and improve consistency.

Advanced Reflection

Flow is not a passive state; it is an emergent property of skill, awareness, and probabilistic alignment. It requires:

- **Deep Self-Knowledge:** Understanding habitual cognitive and emotional patterns.
- **Probabilistic Literacy:** Comfort with uncertainty and dynamic assessment of probabilities.
- **Continuous Feedback Integration:** Adjusting mental models based on market responses and outcomes.

Insight: Traders in flow often describe time "slowing down" during critical decisions. This subjective expansion allows nuanced probability assessments, reduces impulsivity, and enhances adaptive execution.

Closing Thoughts

Achieving flow transforms trading from reactive survival to conscious navigation of probabilities. Through mindfulness, reflection, probabilistic mapping, and emotional calibration, traders cultivate the ability to perceive market uncertainty as an actionable landscape rather than a source of stress.

Flow is not a fleeting state it is a trainable skill. For advanced traders, mastering flow is equivalent to mastering the probabilistic dance of the market: adaptive, precise, and profoundly effective.

16.2 Awareness-Action Alignment Techniques

Introduction

In probabilistic markets, the gap between awareness and action often determines trading success. Awareness without decisive action results in missed opportunities, while action without awareness leads to errors amplified by emotion and cognitive bias. Aligning perception with behavior ensures that every decision reflects both accurate market reading and calibrated internal states.

This section explores techniques to bridge the observer and actor in trading, integrating mindfulness, probabilistic reasoning, and reflective practices. Advanced traders learn not just to see opportunities, but to act on them coherently and consistently.

The Principle of Alignment

Awareness-action alignment can be summarized as the seamless integration of three layers:

1. **Perceptual Awareness:** Observing market signals with minimal distortion, noting probabilities, trends, and anomalies.

2. **Cognitive Calibration:** Processing observations through mental models that account for uncertainty, biases, and emergent patterns.

3. **Action Execution:** Translating perception and analysis into deliberate, probabilistically-informed trades.

Misalignment occurs when one layer dominates or operates in isolation. For instance, a trader may perceive signals clearly but hesitate due to fear, or act impulsively without fully considering the probability landscape.

Techniques for Awareness-Action Integration

1. Micro-Pause Decision Technique

1. Before executing any trade, take a micro-pause (3-5 seconds) to observe current emotional and cognitive states.
2. Ask: "Am I responding to probability, pattern, or emotion?"
3. Adjust the action plan to ensure alignment with observed probabilities rather than reactive impulses.

2. Probabilistic Intention Setting

1. At the start of each session, define probabilistic intentions: "I will take trades with probability $\geq 65\%$ and risk-reward ≥ 1.5."
2. Link each action to this intention during execution to maintain awareness-action coherence.
3. Reflect post-session to measure adherence and recalibrate thresholds.

3. Emotional-Probability Checklists

1. Maintain a short checklist that reviews both emotional state and market probabilities.
2. Example items: "Emotion: Neutral/High fear/High greed; Probability: 60% chance of breakout; Alignment: Proceed or wait."
3. Use this tool in real time to prevent misaligned actions caused by emotional interference.

4. Iterative Feedback Loops

1. Treat each trade as a micro-experiment: observe, act, reflect.
2. Track deviations between expected probability and outcome.
3. Use feedback to adjust both mental models and execution strategies iteratively.

5. Anchored Awareness Exercises

1. Use physical or mental anchors (breathing, finger touch, visualization) to quickly center awareness before acting.
2. Activate anchors during volatile scenarios to reduce impulsivity and maintain clarity.
3. Over time, anchors create a conditioned pathway linking awareness directly to deliberate, aligned action.

Analogies for Clarity

1. Archery Analogy: A skilled archer does not simply release the arrow randomly; the shot requires focus, breath control, and alignment between observation (target), cognitive calibration (trajectory), and action (release). Misalignment between any of these layers results in a missed shot.

2. Musical Performance Analogy: A pianist reading a complex score must simultaneously perceive notes, interpret dynamics, and execute hand movements precisely. Awareness-action alignment ensures that intention translates into flawless performance.

Reflective Practices

1. **Session Debrief Journaling:** Document not only trade outcomes but also alignment levels: "Was my awareness fully reflected in action? Where did emotion override probability?"

2. **Probability-Emotion Mapping:** Visualize decisions on a two-dimensional chart with probability on one axis and emotional intensity on the other to identify patterns of misalignment.

3. **Scenario Simulation:** Mentally rehearse trades in hypothetical markets, consciously practicing alignment between perception, probability, and action.

Key Takeaways

- Awareness alone is insufficient; action must reflect observed probabilities and calibrated cognitive states.

- Misalignment often manifests as hesitation, impulsivity, or overconfidence.

- Deliberate techniques, micro-pauses, anchored exercises, and reflective practices reinforce the bridge between observation and execution.

- Iterative practice converts awareness-action alignment from an abstract concept into a sustainable trading skill.

Closing Reflection

In probabilistic markets, every action is both an experiment and a statement of awareness. Traders who cultivate awareness-action alignment move beyond reaction and enter a state of conscious adaptability. Here, perception informs action with precision, emotion enhances rather than disrupts, and each decision contributes to a coherent, probabilistically-aligned trading rhythm. Mastery of this alignment is not a destination but a continuous practice a lifelong exercise in harmonizing mind, probability, and market behavior.

16.3 Mind-Market Synchronization Exercises

Introduction

Achieving synchronization between mind and market is the culmination of probabilistic awareness, emotional calibration, and conscious decision-making. This state, often referred to as "flow" in trading, allows the trader to act with clarity, adaptability, and precision amid uncertainty. Synchronization is not a passive state; it is actively cultivated through exercises that align perception, probability, emotion, and action.

These exercises guide the trader to develop a rhythmic interplay between observation, analysis, and execution, ensuring that mental models resonate with the probabilistic patterns of the market.

Exercise 1: Pre-Market Mental Alignment

1. Begin each trading day with a 10–15 minute session of mindful observation. Focus on breathing, heartbeat, and present-moment awareness.
2. Review key market indicators, news, and probability distributions, observing without judgment.
3. Set clear probabilistic intentions for the day: identify trades with high expected probability and define risk-reward boundaries.
4. Visualize executing trades aligned with both probability estimates and emotional calm.
5. Outcome: This exercise primes the mind to enter the market in a state of coherence, reducing the risk of reactive decisions.

Exercise 2: Real-Time Awareness Calibration

1. During trading, periodically pause to assess emotional intensity, cognitive load, and perceptual clarity.
2. Map each observation to a probability estimate: "Given the current signals, the probability of my expected outcome is 65%."
3. If awareness and intended action are misaligned (e.g., high fear influencing position sizing), employ an anchor such as a deep breath or a short visualization to recalibrate.
4. Outcome: Traders maintain alignment between internal state and external probabilities, reducing impulsivity and error.

Exercise 3: Synchronization with Market Rhythms

1. Track short-term market cycles (price oscillations, volume surges) and note patterns of recurrence.

2. Attempt to anticipate the next probabilistic movement without committing capital; simply observe and mentally map possible outcomes.

3. Engage in mock execution: imagine how you would act if the market moved along predicted paths.

4. Outcome: Builds intuitive resonance with market rhythms and strengthens the mind's anticipatory capabilities.

Exercise 4: Probability-Emotion Coupling

1. For each potential trade or market scenario, rate both the probability of success and the intensity of emotional response (fear, excitement, hope).

2. Compare emotional intensity against probability estimates; adjust action plans to reflect rational probabilistic alignment rather than emotional bias.

3. Practice repeated cycles of this mapping during both simulated and live markets.

4. Outcome: Cultivates the ability to maintain emotional equilibrium while acting on high-probability opportunities.

Exercise 5: Post-Session Reflective Resonance

1. After the trading session, journal not only outcomes but also internal states at key decision points.

2. Identify patterns of alignment and misalignment: moments when perception, probability assessment, emotion, and action were coherent versus discordant.

3. Reflect on triggers, feedback loops, and decision dynamics to recalibrate future behavior.

4. Outcome: Creates meta-awareness, reinforcing synchronization over time and enhancing probabilistic intuition.

Analogies for Deep Understanding

1. Dancing with the Market: Synchronization resembles a skilled dance, where one partner leads but both are attuned to each other's subtle shifts. Traders "move" with the market's rhythm, adjusting strategy and execution in real time, responding fluidly to changes in probability waves.

2. Sailing the Probabilistic Seas: The market is an ocean of uncertainty. The trader, like a seasoned sailor, adjusts sails and rudder to harness currents rather than fight them. Awareness-action alignment ensures that responses are adaptive, not reactive, and that risk is managed with fluid intelligence.

Key Principles for Effective Synchronization

- **Continuous Awareness:** Maintain a real-time sense of both external market probabilities and internal emotional states.
- **Dynamic Adjustment:** Treat every trade as an opportunity to recalibrate perception-action alignment.
- **Iterative Learning:** Post-session reflection and journaling transform experience into actionable insight.
- **Anchored Attention:** Use physical, mental, or ritual anchors to quickly return to a coherent state during high-volatility events.
- **Meta-Awareness:** Develop the capacity to observe your own observation being aware of how your mind perceives probability, interprets signals, and biases action.

Closing Reflection

Mind-market synchronization is the embodiment of conscious, probabilistic trading. It transforms observation into action, uncertainty into opportunity, and emotional turbulence into adaptive insight. The exercises outlined cultivate a rhythm in which awareness, probability, and decision-making coalesce, allowing the trader to act with precision, confidence, and resilience. In this state, trading is no longer a mechanical response to market noise but a deliberate, flowing interplay between consciousness and probabilistic reality.

Chapter 17

Risk and Uncertainty as Allies

In financial markets, risk and uncertainty are often perceived as adversaries threats to be minimized or avoided. Yet, for the advanced trader, risk is not merely a hazard; it is a source of information, a carrier of probabilistic energy that can be harnessed strategically. This chapter explores the reframing of risk and uncertainty as allies, transforming them from external pressures into active components of conscious trading.

We begin by understanding risk as a probabilistic quantity, influenced not only by market dynamics but also by perception, attention, and emotional calibration. By viewing risk through a quantum-inspired lens, traders can leverage uncertainty to identify opportunities, adjust position sizing, and align decision-making with market probability waves.

17.1 Reframing Risk as Probabilistic Energy

In traditional trading paradigms, risk is often treated as a negative quantity a hazard to be minimized or avoided. However, when viewed through a probabilistic and consciousness-informed lens, risk transforms into a form of energy: dynamic, informative, and actionable. It is not simply a measure of potential loss but a signal reflecting the probabilities of multiple market outcomes, filtered through perception, cognition, and emotion.

The Dual Nature of Risk

Risk embodies a dual character: it carries both danger and information. Consider a market scenario where an asset's price is highly volatile. To a reactive trader, this volatility signals danger. To a probabilistic thinker, volatility reveals uncertainty, which can be quantified, interpreted, and even leveraged.

Analogy: Imagine standing near a river with strong currents. Risk is not just the threat of being swept away; it is also the river's flow, indicating direction, speed, and the best path for navigation. Similarly, market uncertainty can guide a trader toward probabilistically favorable opportunities if interpreted consciously.

Probabilistic Energy in Practice

Every trade contains embedded probabilistic energy. This energy manifests as:

- **Price Range Potential:** The spectrum of likely price movements given historical, technical, and behavioral data.
- **Event Sensitivity:** How macroeconomic releases, geopolitical events, or company-specific news influence probabilities.
- **Emotional Flux:** Traders' collective emotional states amplify or dampen market responses, creating dynamic probabilistic fields.

Recognizing these factors allows traders to quantify risk not as a static metric but as a dynamic probability cloud an energy field to observe, measure, and interact with.

Transforming Perception of Risk

To shift perception from fear-based to probabilistic energy, traders can adopt the following strategies:

1. **Label Probabilities Instead of Losses:** Before entering a trade, mentally articulate the probabilities of each scenario (e.g., 40% up, 50% neutral, 10% down), rather than fixating on potential monetary loss. This reframing converts abstract risk into measurable energy.
2. **Observe Emotional Resonance:** Notice how fear, greed, or hope fluctuates in response to perceived probabilities. Treat emotional reactions as indicators of where your perception may be misaligned with actual probabilistic fields.
3. **Align Position Size with Probabilistic Energy:** Use calculated probabilities to scale positions. Higher certainty (more concentrated probability distribution) may warrant greater allocation, whereas diffuse probabilities suggest smaller, cautious exposure.
4. **Feedback and Iteration:** Post-trade reflection helps calibrate perception of risk energy against actual outcomes. Over time, this develops intuition for probabilistic flow.

Practical Exercise: Mapping Probabilistic Energy

1. Identify a set of potential trades for the coming week.
2. For each trade, assign subjective probabilities to multiple outcomes.
3. Note your emotional response to each scenario, highlighting potential overreaction or underestimation.
4. Allocate position sizes according to probability-weighted expected outcomes.
5. After the trading session, reflect on actual results versus your probability map, refining your internal calibration.

Philosophical Reflection

Risk, reframed as probabilistic energy, is inseparable from consciousness. It exists not as an external adversary but as a relational phenomenon between trader, perception, and market. By perceiving risk as a dynamic signal, traders can harmonize intuition, probability, and action transforming uncertainty from a source of anxiety into a guide for strategic decision-making.

In essence, the trader's mastery emerges not from eliminating risk, but from learning to sense, interpret, and channel its energy toward probabilistically aligned, conscious action.

17.2 Resonant Position Sizing and Scaling

In probabilistic trading, position sizing is not simply a function of capital allocation or risk limits; it is a dynamic resonance with the probabilistic energy present in the market. When a trader aligns position size with both the likelihood of outcomes and their internal awareness, the result is a coherent, adaptive engagement with market uncertainty.

The Concept of Resonant Sizing

Resonant position sizing treats each trade as an interaction with a probability field. Rather than committing a fixed proportion of capital, the trader adjusts exposure in proportion to:

- **Certainty of Outcome:** Sharper probability distributions allow more confident sizing, while diffuse distributions suggest smaller exposure.
- **Emotional Calibration:** Awareness of internal emotional states prevents overleveraging during excitement or underinvestment during hesitation.

- **Market Context:** Volatility, liquidity, and correlations with other positions inform how much energy to commit to a particular probabilistic scenario.

Analogy: Consider a musician tuning an instrument to resonate with an orchestra. Over-tightening a string produces dissonance, while undertension results in weak projection. Similarly, the trader tunes position sizes to harmonize with the probabilistic and emotional "orchestra" of the market.

Scaling in Probabilistic Markets

Scaling refers to dynamically adjusting position size as probabilities and market conditions evolve. Instead of static entries and exits, traders incrementally scale into or out of positions, guided by real-time observation of probabilistic energy.

1. **Incremental Entries:** Entering a position in stages allows the trader to respond to unfolding market evidence and refine probabilistic estimates.

2. **Adaptive Exits:** Scaling out of positions according to emerging probability shifts minimizes the impact of unforeseen volatility.

3. **Hedging via Scaling:** Partial hedges or counter-balancing positions can be layered based on real-time feedback from probability distributions, enhancing coherence between exposure and market energy.

Practical Framework for Resonant Positioning

1. **Step 1: Quantify Probabilities** Assign subjective probabilities to each potential outcome of a trade.

2. **Step 2: Evaluate Market Resonance** Observe volatility, correlations, and emotional state to determine initial exposure.

3. **Step 3: Determine Base Position Size** Scale capital proportional to probabilistic certainty and internal calibration.

4. **Step 4: Adjust Dynamically** As probabilities shift due to new data or price movement, modify exposure incrementally to remain in resonance with the evolving market state.

5. **Step 5: Reflect and Refine** Post-trade analysis of sizing decisions reinforces internal calibration and probabilistic intuition.

Illustrative Example

Imagine a trader analyzing a stock with the following subjective probabilities:

- 50% chance of a 5% gain
- 30% chance of a 2% loss
- 20% chance of a 10% loss

The trader's internal awareness suggests moderate confidence and a calm emotional state. A resonant sizing approach may allocate a larger initial position corresponding to the 50% positive scenario, while leaving room to scale in or hedge as new market information unfolds.

This method contrasts with rigid "fixed fraction" sizing, which ignores the fluid interplay between probability, perception, and market dynamics.

Philosophical Reflection

Resonant position sizing embodies the principle that trading is an interaction, not a conquest. By calibrating exposure to the probabilistic energy of both markets and mind, the trader transforms risk into aligned action. Scaling, like a symphony crescendo, allows the trader to amplify advantage when resonance is high and temper it when uncertainty dominates.

Exercises for Mastery

1. **Probability-Weighted Sizing Drill** Select multiple trades, assign probabilities, and practice determining scaled position sizes according to probabilistic energy and emotional calibration.

2. **Dynamic Scaling Simulation** Using historical price data, simulate scaling into positions based on evolving probabilities, reflecting on how incremental adjustments affect coherence and risk management.

3. **Reflective Journaling** Document both the quantitative reasoning and qualitative perception behind sizing decisions, reinforcing alignment between mind, market, and probabilistic assessment.

Through resonant position sizing and adaptive scaling, traders cultivate the ability to navigate uncertainty with precision, integrating intuition, probability, and awareness into every market engagement.

17.3 Adaptive Risk Management Models

Traditional risk management often relies on static rules fixed stop-losses, position caps, or predetermined risk-per-trade percentages. While these methods provide a baseline structure, they fail to capture the dynamic, probabilistic nature of markets, especially when human perception, collective behavior, and uncertainty interact. Adaptive risk management transforms rigid rules into flexible frameworks that evolve with market conditions, internal awareness, and probabilistic assessments.

Principles of Adaptive Risk Management

Adaptive models are guided by several core principles:

- **Dynamic Probability Assessment:** Risk exposure adjusts according to evolving probability distributions rather than fixed assumptions.
- **Emotional and Cognitive Calibration:** The trader's internal state informs risk tolerance; heightened stress or overconfidence triggers proportionally reduced exposure.
- **Feedback-Driven Adjustments:** Market signals, trade outcomes, and observed behavioral patterns feed continuously into the risk model, creating a self-correcting loop.
- **Scenario Flexibility:** Adaptive frameworks account for multiple possible market states, including rare but impactful tail events, rather than only expected outcomes.

Integrating Probabilistic Energy into Risk Models

In a probabilistic framework, risk is not a static number but a dynamic field of potential outcomes. Traders can quantify this "probabilistic energy" using techniques such as:

- Assigning subjective probabilities to scenarios based on analysis and observation.
- Measuring volatility and correlation dynamics to gauge exposure sensitivity.
- Evaluating potential drawdowns weighted by probability distributions, not solely historical maxima.

Analogy: Consider a surfer navigating shifting waves. A fixed stance may work on one wave but fails on another. Adaptive balance adjusting weight, angle, and timing maximizes the ride while minimizing the risk of wipeout. Similarly, an adaptive risk model adjusts positions, stops, and hedges in real-time to maintain coherence with the probabilistic market landscape.

Components of an Adaptive Model

1. **Dynamic Exposure Scaling:** Position sizes expand or contract in proportion to probability confidence and market volatility.
2. **Probabilistic Stop-Losses:** Instead of arbitrary stop levels, stops are determined by the likelihood of adverse movements exceeding tolerable thresholds.
3. **Hedging and Diversification:** Risk is mitigated through layered hedges, correlated assets, and counterbalancing positions, scaled according to real-time correlations and probability shifts.
4. **Continuous Feedback Analysis:** Post-trade reflection, journaling, and quantitative review feed back into model parameters to improve predictive coherence.

Illustrative Example

Suppose a trader identifies two correlated assets, A and B. Asset A shows high probabilistic confidence for a favorable move, while asset B is more volatile with uncertain outcomes. Using an adaptive model:

- Increase exposure to asset A proportional to confidence.
- Scale exposure to asset B cautiously, with probabilistic stop-losses and optional hedges.
- Continuously reassess as price action unfolds, adjusting position sizes and risk thresholds in response to real-time probabilistic feedback.

This approach contrasts sharply with rigid models that would either allocate equally to both assets or rely on fixed stop percentages, ignoring evolving market energy and trader awareness.

Philosophical Reflection

Markets are living systems, not static machines. Adaptive risk management treats each trade as an interaction with a probabilistic environment, acknowledging uncertainty as an ally rather than a threat. By continuously integrating perception, probability, and internal calibration, traders align their risk exposure with the flow of market energy, enhancing both survival and opportunity in complex environments.

Exercises for Mastery

1. **Probability-Weighted Risk Assessment:** Select a set of trades and assign probabilities to outcomes. Determine adaptive position sizes and stop-losses based on probabilistic energy rather than fixed percentages.

2. **Dynamic Scaling Simulation:** Using historical or simulated data, practice adjusting exposure dynamically as probabilities and correlations shift.

3. **Reflective Journaling:** Document decisions, exposure adjustments, and probabilistic reasoning. Review how adaptive changes affected outcomes and internal coherence.

4. **Stress Testing:** Simulate rare market events and evaluate whether adaptive adjustments preserved capital and coherence under extreme uncertainty.

Adaptive risk management is more than a technical discipline it is a philosophy of engagement with uncertainty. By embedding probabilistic thinking, emotional calibration, and iterative feedback into the risk framework, traders convert uncertainty from an adversary into a navigable, actionable field of opportunity.

Chapter 18

Observing Market Waves

Markets are rarely linear; they move in waves, pulses, and patterns that emerge from the collective actions of countless participants. Each price movement is a probabilistic signal, a reflection of perception, expectation, and latent potential. To trade effectively, one must develop the ability to observe these waves with clarity, discerning meaningful patterns from transient noise.

The Philosophy of Market Observation

Observing markets is more than monitoring price charts; it is cultivating a heightened awareness of probabilistic dynamics. By attuning to subtle shifts, correlations, and recurring structures, traders gain insight into underlying market energy. Observation involves both cognitive precision and emotional stability the mind must see without distortion, and the emotions must calibrate to probabilistic reality rather than reactive impulses.

18.1 Detecting Probabilistic Market Patterns

Markets are, at their core, probabilistic systems. Every price movement represents a convergence of countless decisions, expectations, and reactions, each with its own inherent uncertainty. To the untrained eye, these movements may appear random, chaotic, or inscrutable. Yet, hidden within this apparent chaos are recurring probabilistic patterns structures born from human behavior, institutional strategies, and the rhythmic oscillations of supply and demand. Detecting these patterns requires both rigorous observation and a nuanced understanding of probability.

Understanding Patterns Beyond Determinism

Traditional technical analysis often treats charts as deterministic: a pattern forms, and a predefined outcome follows. In probabilistic thinking, however, patterns do not guarantee outcomes; they indicate likelihoods. A "head-and-shoulders" formation is not a prophecy it is a probabilistic signal that certain market behaviors are more likely given the observed structure. Traders who detect patterns with this mindset avoid the trap of certainty, embracing the fluidity and uncertainty inherent in markets.

Example: Consider a sudden spike in volume accompanied by a breakout above resistance. Instead of assuming the breakout will continue indefinitely, a probabilistic approach evaluates the likelihood of continuation versus retracement. Factors such as prior volatility, broader market sentiment, and correlated asset behavior are incorporated into this probabilistic assessment.

Cognitive Tools for Pattern Detection

Effective detection of probabilistic patterns relies on the integration of perception, memory, and probabilistic reasoning:

1. **Pattern Recognition Memory:** Build a mental library of recurring market behaviors, noting the conditions under which they manifest and the typical probabilistic outcomes. This is not rote memorization but experiential encoding of probabilities across multiple contexts.

2. **Contextual Awareness:** Every pattern exists within a broader probabilistic landscape. A breakout in a trending market differs from one in a range-bound environment. Integrating context allows the trader to weight the probability of outcomes accurately.

3. **Probability Visualization:** Visualize each observed pattern as a probability cloud a range of potential outcomes with varying likelihoods. This mental exercise strengthens the connection between perception and probabilistic judgment.

Practical Reflection: Observing Probabilities in Real-Time

Traders often report that patterns "emerge" when they step back from reactive behavior and allow a probabilistic lens to guide observation. This involves:

- Watching price action without impulsively trading on the first signal.
- Mentally assigning likelihoods to potential outcomes.
- Tracking how these probabilities evolve as new data arrives.

Exercise: Probability Mapping of Patterns

1. Select three recurring patterns observed in your preferred market.

2. For each pattern, assign a subjective probability distribution for likely outcomes (e.g., continuation, retracement, reversal).
3. Observe subsequent price action and compare with your initial probability map.
4. Record deviations, insights, and emotional responses in a trading journal. Over time, this refines both pattern detection and probabilistic reasoning.

Philosophical Insight

Detecting probabilistic patterns is as much an art as a science. The market does not reveal its secrets through linear logic alone; it communicates through waves, correlations, and emergent structures. A trader attuned to these signals is simultaneously observer and participant, perceiving the probabilities while respecting the uncertainty. Over time, this practice cultivates an intuitive sense of market rhythm a flow of perception and probabilistic insight that supports adaptive, conscious trading decisions.

Integrating Emotional Calibration

Even the most precise probabilistic assessment can be compromised if emotional states distort perception. Fear may exaggerate risk; greed may inflate perceived probability of favorable outcomes. Detecting patterns effectively requires emotional equilibrium, where observation is guided by awareness rather than reaction. Integrating real-time emotional calibration with probabilistic detection strengthens both accuracy and confidence in decision-making.

By combining perceptual acuity, probabilistic reasoning, and emotional calibration, traders transform pattern detection from mechanical observation into an active dialogue with the market. Each observed wave, volume shift, or price structure becomes a probabilistic signal, providing guidance without guaranteeing outcomes allowing the trader to act with clarity, flexibility, and adaptive intelligence.

18.2 Cognitive and Emotional Calibration

Effective trading is not solely a matter of technical skill or market knowledge; it is fundamentally a practice of calibrating the mind. Cognitive and emotional calibration refers to the process of aligning perception, thought, and feeling to navigate probabilistic markets with clarity and precision. Without this alignment, even the most sophisticated models and pattern recognition strategies can be undermined by bias, overreaction, or hesitation.

The Role of Cognitive Calibration

Cognitive calibration involves honing the mind's ability to accurately perceive probabilities, recognize patterns, and make decisions consistent with observed evidence. Key components include:

1. **Awareness of Mental Biases:** Traders must recognize cognitive distortions such as confirmation bias, recency bias, or overconfidence. Awareness is the first step in mitigating their influence on probabilistic judgment.

2. **Adaptive Probabilistic Thinking:** Rather than assuming a deterministic outcome, the calibrated mind evaluates multiple potential scenarios, weighting them according to likelihood and context. This allows the trader to anticipate both favorable and unfavorable outcomes without emotional overreaction.

3. **Metacognitive Reflection:** Periodically reviewing thought processes enhances self-awareness. Questions like "Am I reacting or observing?" or "How are my assumptions shaping my probability estimates?" cultivate a reflective mindset, preventing automatic or habitual errors.

Example: A trader observing a breakout may feel an urge to immediately enter a position due to excitement or fear of missing out. Through cognitive calibration, the trader pauses, assesses the probabilistic likelihood of continuation versus retracement, and decides based on the relative probabilities rather than impulsive emotion.

The Role of Emotional Calibration

Emotions serve as both signals and filters. Fear, greed, hope, or frustration can distort perception of probabilities and risk. Emotional calibration ensures that the mind interprets market signals accurately without being hijacked by transient affective states. Core practices include:

- **Emotional Labeling:** Identifying and naming emotions in real-time helps prevent unconscious reactions. For instance, acknowledging "I feel anxious due to recent losses" allows conscious adjustment.

- **Intensity Regulation:** Employing breathing, mindfulness, or visualization techniques modulates emotional intensity, maintaining a stable internal environment for decision-making.

- **Integration with Cognitive Assessment:** Emotional calibration should inform rather than override probabilistic thinking. Recognizing the influence of emotions on subjective probabilities allows traders to adjust their estimates with greater accuracy.

Practical Exercises for Calibration

Exercise 1: Cognitive Bias Tracking

1. Maintain a trading journal specifically focused on cognitive biases.
2. After each session, identify instances where biases may have influenced decisions.
3. Reflect on alternative probabilistic assessments that could have been applied.

Exercise 2: Emotional Awareness Mapping

1. During live trading, periodically pause to record dominant emotions and intensity levels.
2. Note how each emotion affects perception of risk and probability estimates.
3. Implement micro-adjustments in exposure or strategy to counteract distortions.

Exercise 3: Scenario Simulation with Cognitive-Emotional Integration

1. Mentally simulate market scenarios with varying degrees of volatility and uncertainty.
2. For each scenario, anticipate likely emotional responses.
3. Pair these anticipated emotions with calibrated probabilistic decisions.
4. Debrief post-simulation to refine both cognitive and emotional calibration.

Philosophical Reflection

Markets are mirrors of collective human behavior. The trader's mind, as both observer and participant, is inseparably linked to the probabilistic dynamics it seeks to navigate. Calibration cognitive and emotional is the process of harmonizing internal perception with external uncertainty. It transforms trading from reactive guessing into conscious, adaptive interaction with market probability waves.

Closing Thoughts

Cognitive and emotional calibration is the foundation upon which all advanced trading practices rest. By integrating reflective awareness, bias mitigation, and emotional modulation, traders cultivate a resilient, adaptive mindset. This mental alignment not only improves probabilistic accuracy but also fosters composure, strategic clarity, and sustainable performance. In essence, calibration allows the trader to perceive, interpret, and act in harmony with the fluid, probabilistic reality of financial markets.

18.3 Practical Observation Exercises

Observation is the bridge between perception and informed action. In probabilistic markets, the quality of your observations directly influences the accuracy of probability estimates, the alignment of decisions with market dynamics, and the effectiveness of risk management. Practical observation exercises train both cognitive and emotional faculties, sharpening awareness and enabling traders to detect subtle patterns in price action, volume, and collective behavior.

Exercise 1: Multi-Timescale Observation

1. Select a financial instrument and observe its price action across multiple timescales (e.g., 1-minute, 15-minute, daily charts).
2. Record key patterns, support/resistance levels, and volatility signals at each timescale.
3. Compare observations across scales to identify where local fluctuations align or conflict with broader trends.
4. Reflect on how temporal perspective influences probabilistic judgments and emotional responses.

Insight: Markets often behave differently across timescales. Recognizing coherence or divergence across scales allows the trader to better anticipate short-term volatility within a long-term trend, aligning both cognitive assessment and emotional expectation.

Exercise 2: Emotional-Perceptual Checkpoints

1. During trading sessions, pause at regular intervals to assess both external market signals and internal emotional states.
2. Ask questions such as: "Am I observing the market objectively, or reacting emotionally?"
3. Note discrepancies between perception and emotional state.
4. Adjust your approach: either recalibrate emotionally or refine observation to reduce bias.

Analogy: Just as a pilot regularly checks instruments to ensure accurate navigation, a trader must periodically check internal "instruments" of perception and emotion to maintain alignment with market reality.

Exercise 3: Probabilistic Pattern Journaling

1. Maintain a dedicated journal for probabilistic observations.
2. For each trading session, record patterns, signals, and any deviations from expected probabilities.
3. Annotate your emotional reactions and decisions at critical junctures.
4. Over time, identify recurring patterns in both the market and your cognitive-emotional responses.
5. Use this meta-awareness to refine probability estimates and decision-making frameworks.

Exercise 4: Blind Observation Drills

1. Choose a market or instrument and turn off all predictive indicators or charts that suggest outcomes.
2. Observe only price movement, volume, and order flow.
3. Record your observations without forming immediate conclusions.
4. After a set period, reflect on your initial perceptions versus actual market behavior.
5. This strengthens raw observational skills, reducing over-reliance on preconceived models.

Exercise 5: Collective Behavior Mapping

1. Observe multiple correlated instruments simultaneously to detect synchronized movements, divergence, or anomalous behavior.
2. Document instances where collective patterns suggest underlying market sentiment or institutional positioning.
3. Reflect on how these collective observations inform your probabilistic assessment and strategic positioning.

Philosophical Reflection

Observation in markets is not passive; it is an active engagement with probability, uncertainty, and human behavior. By systematically practicing multi-timescale awareness, emotional-perceptual checks, journaling, blind observation, and collective mapping, traders develop a heightened sensitivity to subtle signals. Observation becomes both a cognitive skill and an emotional discipline, fostering clarity, composure, and adaptive insight.

Closing Thoughts

Practical observation exercises serve as the training ground for conscious, probabilistic trading. They cultivate the capacity to notice patterns without premature judgment, to align perception with probability, and to integrate emotional awareness into decision-making. Through consistent practice, the trader transforms from a reactive participant into a perceptive observer and deliberate actor, capable of synchronizing mind, market, and probability in a continuous feedback loop.

Chapter 19

Decision Mastery Under Uncertainty

In probabilistic markets, uncertainty is not an obstacle it is the medium in which opportunity and insight emerge. Every decision involves balancing conflicting probabilities, integrating incomplete information, and navigating the interplay between cognitive evaluation and emotional response. Mastery under uncertainty requires both conceptual clarity and practical flexibility: the ability to hold multiple potential outcomes simultaneously, to update beliefs dynamically, and to act decisively without collapsing under the weight of ambiguity.

This chapter explores strategies and exercises for cultivating advanced decision-making capabilities in real-time trading. It emphasizes mental superposition the capacity to consider, weigh, and adapt to several probable outcomes at once while maintaining composure and strategic clarity. Through reflective practice and targeted exercises, traders learn to expand cognitive flexibility, reduce bias, and synchronize awareness with market dynamics.

19.1 Balancing Conflicting Probabilities

In financial markets, conflicting probabilities are the norm rather than the exception. Every trade is embedded within a web of interdependent outcomes, where multiple signals, indicators, and narratives point in different directions. Successful traders do not seek certainty they learn to balance these conflicting probabilities, integrating objective analysis with subjective perception, and maintaining composure amidst ambiguity.

Conceptual Overview

Consider the market as a probabilistic landscape: every potential price movement carries an associated likelihood, influenced by macroeconomic data, technical patterns, and collective trader sentiment. Conflicting probabilities arise when different sources suggest opposing directions. For example, a technical indicator may suggest an upward trend while news events or sentiment analysis suggest increased downside risk.

Balancing these probabilities requires understanding that each signal is not a guarantee but a weighted input into a broader probabilistic model. Rather than attempting to isolate a single "correct" outcome, traders maintain a probabilistic perspective, assigning confidence levels to each scenario and continuously updating these weights as new information emerges.

Analogical Insight

Visualize a tightrope walker navigating a rope in the wind. The walker senses gusts from all directions simultaneously. Each gust is not a certainty but a force with varying magnitude and direction. Success requires perceiving all forces, calibrating responses to their combined effect, and maintaining balance without overreacting to any single gust. In trading, the "gusts" are conflicting probabilities, and the trader's balance is achieved through measured, probabilistically informed decision-making.

Practical Techniques

1. **Probability Weighting:** Assign explicit numerical probabilities to each potential outcome based on evidence. For example, a technical signal might carry a 60% likelihood of upward movement, while sentiment suggests 40% probability of a downward move. Updating these weights dynamically keeps decisions aligned with reality.

2. **Scenario Integration:** Construct multiple scenarios, each representing a combination of potential outcomes. For each scenario, evaluate expected value, risk exposure, and emotional response. This helps reconcile conflicting inputs into actionable insight.

3. **Weighted Decision Trees:** Visualize outcomes as branches of a tree, with probability-weighted expected values at each node. This forces clarity about trade-offs and highlights which scenarios dominate risk-reward considerations.

4. **Signal Prioritization:** Identify which signals have historically carried higher predictive validity in specific contexts. Use these as anchors to balance less certain or noisier signals, without ignoring them entirely.

5. **Reflective Pause:** When probabilities conflict sharply, implement a conscious pause. During this pause, review all weighted inputs, ask

what has changed since the last assessment, and check for emotional bias. This mitigates impulsive decisions under uncertainty.

Exercises for Mastery

1. **Dual-Signal Journaling:** For each trading session, select two conflicting indicators. Document the probabilities you assign to each outcome, and track the actual market movement. Reflect on how your weighting influenced decisions and identify patterns in bias or misjudgment.
2. **Scenario Overlay Drill:** Create three opposing market scenarios with assigned probabilities. Simulate decision-making by evaluating risk, reward, and exposure for each scenario. Repeat under different market conditions to reinforce adaptive weighting skills.
3. **Emotional Calibration Check:** During sessions with high-conflict probabilities, rate emotional intensity and compare it to the probabilities you assigned. Train awareness of when fear, greed, or hope may distort weighting.

Philosophical Reflection

Balancing conflicting probabilities is a practice in humility and patience. It requires acknowledging that no single model or signal holds absolute truth, and that mastery lies in harmonizing multiple perspectives. Like a symphony conductor balancing diverse instruments, the trader orchestrates probabilities into a coherent, adaptive framework, transforming uncertainty into informed action.

Key Takeaways

- Conflicting probabilities are inevitable; the goal is to integrate them effectively rather than eliminate them.
- Explicitly weighting outcomes and constructing scenario-based frameworks enhances clarity and decision quality.
- Emotional awareness is essential to prevent bias from distorting probability assessments.
- Practice, journaling, and reflective exercises are crucial for developing the skill of balancing probabilities under uncertainty.

19.2 Mental Superposition in Real-Time Trading

In the fast-paced world of financial markets, traders frequently encounter situations where multiple outcomes are simultaneously plausible. Mental superposition is the ability to hold these competing possibilities in mind without prematurely collapsing them into a single, rigid expectation. Mastery of this skill allows traders to navigate uncertainty with clarity, agility, and probabilistic precision.

Conceptual Framework

Borrowing from quantum-inspired thinking, mental superposition does not imply uncertainty or indecision; rather, it emphasizes parallel consideration of all viable outcomes. Just as a quantum particle exists in multiple states until observed, the market presents a spectrum of potential price trajectories, each with its own probability. The trader's task is to maintain awareness of this spectrum, dynamically updating likelihoods as new information arrives, while avoiding the cognitive trap of overcommitment to one perceived outcome.

Analogical Insight

Consider a chess grandmaster contemplating several moves simultaneously. Each branch of potential play leads to different positions, counter-moves, and strategic opportunities. The master visualizes these possibilities in parallel, assessing probabilities, risks, and rewards before selecting the optimal move. In trading, the "chessboard" is the market, and the moves are potential trades or positions, with real-time price fluctuations and external news acting as opposing players.

Practical Implementation

1. **Outcome Mapping:** For any active trade or market scenario, list all plausible outcomes along with subjective probability estimates. Include upside, downside, and neutral scenarios. Continuously update these probabilities as market dynamics evolve.

2. **Parallel Scenario Evaluation:** Mentally simulate multiple price paths and corresponding strategic responses. Assess exposure, stop levels, and potential adjustments for each path without prematurely committing to a single "expected" outcome.

3. **Dynamic Positioning:** Maintain flexibility in position sizing and hedging to reflect the spectrum of possibilities. Avoid over-leveraging based on one scenario; instead, structure positions to accommodate alternative outcomes concurrently.

4. **Emotional Modulation:** Recognize that holding multiple possibilities can induce cognitive tension or stress. Apply emotional calibration techniques, such as controlled breathing or brief mindfulness checks, to prevent anxiety from collapsing superposition into reactive decisions.

Exercises for Mental Superposition

1. **Multi-Scenario Journaling:** For each trade, document three to five potential outcomes and assign probability weights. After market resolution, reflect on how well your superpositioned assessment captured reality and where adjustments are needed.

2. **Simulation Drills:** Using historical price data or paper trading platforms, simulate trades under uncertain conditions. Intentionally maintain multiple plausible hypotheses and avoid acting until probabilities meaningfully shift. Evaluate decision quality and stress response.

3. **Mindfulness Integration:** Before engaging with live markets, perform a brief meditation focusing on observing uncertainty without attachment. Practice recognizing fleeting judgments and gently returning attention to the spectrum of possibilities, reinforcing cognitive flexibility.

Narrative Insight

Advanced traders often describe mental superposition as the difference between reactive trading and adaptive flow. One trader, monitoring a volatile earnings announcement, held simultaneous expectations of both a bullish and bearish market reaction. Instead of prematurely committing to a single direction, she adjusted position sizes to remain neutral, monitored unfolding price movements, and executed actions only when probabilistic clarity emerged. The result was strategic agility, reduced emotional volatility, and superior probabilistic alignment.

Philosophical Reflection

Mental superposition embodies the art of embracing uncertainty without succumbing to paralysis. It teaches traders to inhabit the space between possibilities, cultivating awareness, patience, and adaptability. By recognizing that the market exists in a superposed state until decisions are enacted, traders align their cognition with the probabilistic nature of reality, transforming ambiguity into an instrument of insight rather than a source of anxiety.

Key Takeaways

- Real-time trading inherently involves multiple simultaneous outcomes; mental superposition allows traders to navigate them effectively.

- Parallel consideration of scenarios enhances decision quality, prevents overcommitment, and supports adaptive risk management.

- Exercises in journaling, simulation, and mindfulness strengthen the capacity for superposition and probabilistic alignment.

- Mastery of mental superposition fosters clarity, composure, and agility in dynamic market environments.

19.3 Advanced Flexibility Exercises

In probabilistic markets, flexibility is the trader's most powerful tool. While technical skills and probabilistic reasoning provide the structure for decision-making, true mastery arises from cognitive and emotional flexibility the ability to adapt rapidly, reassess probabilities, and modify actions in real time. This section presents exercises designed to cultivate advanced mental, emotional, and probabilistic flexibility.

Exercise 1: Multi-Hypothesis Trading Drill

1. Select a live or simulated market scenario with multiple plausible outcomes.

2. Identify at least three competing hypotheses for market movement, assigning initial subjective probabilities.

3. Plan trade strategies for each hypothesis, including position sizing, stop levels, and exit conditions.

4. During execution, continuously update probabilities based on incoming data, adjusting exposure accordingly.

5. After completion, analyze decisions: how quickly were probabilities updated? Did cognitive flexibility prevent premature commitment?

Exercise 2: Rapid Scenario Switching

1. During a trading session, deliberately practice shifting mental focus between different timeframes, instruments, or strategies.

2. For each switch, pause to recalibrate probabilities and reassess risk.

3. Observe emotional responses frustration, attachment to prior positions, or inertia and apply emotional regulation techniques to maintain clarity.

4. This exercise strengthens the mind's ability to remain agile under real-time pressure, preventing rigidity in high-stakes environments.

Exercise 3: Contrarian Simulation

1. Identify a prevailing market consensus or "popular trade" scenario.

2. Construct a credible alternative scenario with distinct probabilities and corresponding trade strategies.

3. Execute paper trades or simulations based on both the consensus and the alternative scenario, practicing equal engagement with both.

4. Reflect on cognitive biases such as herd mentality, anchoring, or overconfidence, and note how awareness of these biases enhances probabilistic flexibility.

Exercise 4: Emotional-State Switching

1. Before trading, identify two contrasting emotional states for example, cautious versus opportunistic.

2. Engage in simulated trading scenarios while intentionally adopting each state.

3. Compare decision outcomes, emotional reactivity, and probability assessment accuracy between states.

4. Purpose: cultivate awareness of how emotional flexibility impacts decision-making and market alignment.

Exercise 5: Probability Reassignment Under Stress

1. Introduce unexpected news events or simulated shocks into paper trading sessions.

2. Rapidly reassess probabilities for ongoing trades, accounting for new information.

3. Document both the cognitive process and emotional reactions.

4. Repeat multiple sessions to build the ability to update beliefs and act flexibly under stress, reinforcing adaptive probabilistic thinking.

Narrative Insight

Experienced traders describe advanced flexibility as the difference between reactive rigidity and adaptive flow. One trader, confronted with sudden geopolitical news affecting multiple correlated assets, maintained three concurrent hypotheses for market behavior. By rapidly adjusting position sizes, hedges, and stop-losses while consciously managing emotional reactivity, she navigated uncertainty without panic, ultimately realizing gains and minimizing losses. This illustrates how mental and emotional flexibility translates into tangible trading performance.

Philosophical Reflection

Flexibility is not merely a tactical skill it is a mindset. Markets are dynamic, probabilistic systems where certainty is an illusion. By cultivating cognitive agility, emotional resilience, and probabilistic adaptability, traders align their internal states with external uncertainty. Advanced flexibility exercises transform potential stress and indecision into deliberate, coherent action, allowing traders to move fluidly through the complex interplay of perception, probability, and choice.

Key Takeaways

- Cognitive and emotional flexibility are essential for navigating real-time market uncertainty.
- Exercises such as multi-hypothesis trading, scenario switching, and contrarian simulations enhance adaptive decision-making.
- Emotional awareness and probability reassessment under stress strengthen alignment between perception and market realities.
- Mastering flexibility enables traders to respond with clarity, composure, and probabilistic precision, transforming uncertainty into strategic advantage.

Chapter 20

The Quantum Trader's Mindset

In the final stage of mastering probabilistic markets, the trader evolves from reactive participant to conscious navigator. The Quantum Trader's Mindset integrates awareness, probabilistic reasoning, and flow, enabling decisions that are both adaptive and aligned with market dynamics.

This chapter explores how to synthesize the conceptual frameworks, exercises, and reflective practices from prior chapters into a coherent mindset. It emphasizes not only technical or strategic mastery, but also the cultivation of conscious perception, emotional regulation, and mental flexibility.

We will examine techniques for sustaining mastery through ongoing reflection, deliberate practice, and mindful engagement with uncertainty. Beyond the conventional goals of winning or losing, this mindset positions trading as a practice of alignment with probabilities, market rhythms, and one's own consciousness transforming each trade into an opportunity for growth, insight, and strategic evolution.

Through philosophical reflection, practical exercises, and actionable insights, this chapter guides traders toward a holistic approach where decision-making becomes a conscious art, and market outcomes are interpreted through the lens of perception, probability, and flow.

20.1 Integration of Awareness, Probability, and Flow

Trading at a quantum-conscious level requires more than technical skill or probabilistic calculation it demands the seamless integration of three core faculties: awareness, probability, and flow. Each is a distinct dimension of decision-making, yet their true power emerges only when they are synthesized into a unified approach.

Awareness: The Observer Mind

Awareness is the foundation upon which all conscious trading rests. It is the continuous, non-judgmental observation of both external market dynamics and internal cognitive-emotional states. Without awareness, even the most sophisticated probabilistic models can be misapplied, as bias, emotion, or inattention distorts perception.

Exercise: Mindful Market Observation

1. During each trading session, pause at predefined intervals to note your current thoughts and emotional state.

2. Record market signals you observe without immediately reacting.

3. Reflect on the difference between what is objectively present and how your mind interprets it.

This practice develops the capacity to perceive markets clearly, without the interference of reactive judgments.

Probability: The Language of Uncertainty

Probability allows traders to quantify uncertainty, translating market ambiguity into actionable insights. But probability is not merely numeric; it is also perceptual. Estimating likelihoods requires integrating objective data with subjective intuition honed through experience and reflection.

Example: Probabilistic Scenario Mapping Imagine a stock with multiple potential price movements over the next trading hour. Rather than thinking in absolutes "it will go up" or "it will go down" assign likelihoods to each scenario (e.g., 40% up, 30% neutral, 30% down). Observe how your awareness of the market and your internal state influences these probabilities.

Over time, this practice aligns intuitive perception with objective probabilistic reasoning, creating a mental model that is both flexible and accurate.

Flow: The Harmonization of Mind and Market

Flow represents the state where awareness and probability operate in synchrony with market dynamics. In flow, decision-making is rapid yet measured, intuitive yet informed. Traders experience heightened perception, deep focus, and a sense of effortless alignment with the unfolding probabilistic landscape.

Analogy: Surfing Probabilities Consider a surfer reading the waves. The surfer does not force movement but responds to the natural rhythm, anticipating peaks and troughs. Similarly, in trading, flow arises when awareness and probabilistic reasoning are harmonized, allowing the trader to "ride" market waves rather than fight them.

Integrative Practices for Traders

1. **Pre-Session Alignment:** Before trading, perform a brief meditation or breathing exercise to center attention and enhance awareness.
2. **Probabilistic Visualization:** Mentally simulate multiple trade scenarios and assign probabilities while noting potential emotional responses.
3. **Micro-Flow Checkpoints:** During trading, pause to recalibrate awareness and align decisions with your probabilistic assessment, ensuring flow is maintained.
4. **Post-Session Reflection:** Record not only outcomes but also the degree of alignment among awareness, probability estimation, and flow. Identify patterns of coherence and divergence for continuous improvement.

Philosophical Reflection

Integration is not a linear process but a dynamic dance. Awareness without probabilistic grounding risks indecision; probability without awareness risks misinterpretation; flow without either collapses into reactive behavior. Only when all three dimensions are consciously aligned does the trader access the "quantum" level of market engagement, where each action is informed, adaptable, and harmoniously attuned to the unfolding uncertainty.

Closing Thoughts

The integration of awareness, probability, and flow transforms trading from a mechanical pursuit into a conscious practice. It cultivates clarity, resilience, and strategic adaptability. For advanced traders, this synthesis is the gateway to sustainable mastery, enabling not only profitable decision-making but also the deeper fulfillment that arises from trading with precision, consciousness, and harmony.

20.2 Sustaining Mastery Through Reflection

Mastery in trading is not a static achievement but an evolving state that requires continual reflection. Reflection bridges experience with learning, converting market outcomes, emotional responses, and probabilistic judgments into actionable insight. Without deliberate reflection, even highly skilled traders risk repeating errors, overreacting to market noise, or becoming disconnected from their own awareness and intuition.

The Role of Reflection in Conscious Trading

Reflection serves three essential functions:

1. **Calibration:** Aligning perception, probability, and emotional responses with actual market behavior.
2. **Learning:** Identifying patterns in successes and mistakes, fostering adaptive improvement.
3. **Integration:** Harmonizing cognitive frameworks, mental models, and experiential knowledge into a cohesive decision-making system.

Reflection transforms episodic experiences into structured wisdom, creating a feedback loop that strengthens both skill and self-awareness.

Techniques for Effective Reflection

1. Post-Trade Journaling

After each trading session, record not only trades and outcomes but also your emotional state, cognitive assumptions, and probabilistic estimates. Ask questions such as:

- Did my awareness accurately perceive the market state?
- Were my probability assessments aligned with actual outcomes?
- Which emotional reactions facilitated or hindered decision-making?

This process uncovers hidden biases, reinforces effective strategies, and highlights opportunities for improvement.

2. Pattern Recognition Exercises

Identify recurring behaviors in both market movements and your own responses. For instance, note how sudden spikes in volatility affect decision speed or emotional intensity. Map these patterns across multiple sessions to detect systemic tendencies and refine mental models.

3. Probabilistic Retrospective Analysis

Review trades by reconstructing probability distributions and comparing them to actual outcomes. Reflect on instances where probabilistic assessments were overly confident, overly cautious, or influenced by emotion. This practice strengthens the calibration between subjective perception and objective likelihoods.

Integrating Reflection with Mindful Practice

Reflection is most effective when paired with mindfulness. By observing thoughts and feelings non-judgmentally, traders can disentangle emotion from cognition.

Exercise: Mindful Reflection

1. Choose a recent trade or session.
2. Close your eyes and recall the scenario, noting internal reactions without judgment.
3. Verbally or in writing, describe what you observed, what probabilities you assigned, and how your awareness influenced decisions.
4. Identify lessons and action steps for future sessions.

This combination of mindfulness and structured reflection deepens self-knowledge and reinforces the mental flexibility necessary for high-stakes, probabilistic decision-making.

Narrative Insight

Consider an advanced trader who consistently faced losses in fast-moving markets. Through reflective journaling and probabilistic analysis, she discovered a recurring bias: excessive fear during sharp pullbacks led to premature exits. By combining emotional calibration, flow techniques, and retrospective probability review, she learned to hold positions longer when probabilistic alignment suggested opportunity. Over months, reflection transformed mistakes into adaptive strategies, illustrating the compounding benefits of conscious analysis.

Philosophical Reflection

Reflection elevates trading from a series of transactions to a practice of conscious mastery. It transforms the trader into both observer and participant, creating a continuous loop of awareness, learning, and adaptive action. In this process, success is measured not only in profit but in the refinement of judgment, the harmonization of mind and market, and the cultivation of enduring insight.

Closing Thoughts

Sustaining mastery is an ongoing commitment. Reflection allows traders to internalize lessons, recalibrate probability perception, and refine emotional and cognitive coherence. By embedding reflective practices into daily trading routines, the quantum trader ensures that experience becomes wisdom, mistakes become catalysts for growth, and each decision is informed by the integrated awareness of mind, market, and probability.

20.3 Beyond Winning and Losing: The Philosophy of Conscious Trading

Trading is often framed narrowly as a pursuit of profit, a binary contest of winning or losing. While financial outcomes are tangible and measurable, this perspective neglects the deeper dimensions of trading: the interplay of awareness, decision-making, probability, and emotional coherence. Conscious trading shifts the focus from external results to internal alignment, transforming trading into a practice of mastery rather than mere performance.

Redefining Success

In conscious trading, success is no longer defined solely by financial gain. Instead, it encompasses:

- **Alignment:** Synchronization between perception, probability, and action.
- **Resilience:** Maintaining emotional and cognitive coherence under uncertainty.
- **Adaptability:** Continuously learning from market feedback and evolving circumstances.

By adopting this framework, traders measure their growth not only by P&L statements but also by the quality of decisions, emotional regulation, and clarity of thought.

The Interplay of Mind and Market

Markets are mirrors of collective human behavior, reflecting the sum of beliefs, fears, hopes, and intentions. Conscious trading recognizes that every decision participates in this dynamic system. By cultivating awareness, traders become both observers and contributors, influencing outcomes through probabilistic alignment rather than reactive impulses.

Analogy: Consider the act of surfing. The wave exists independently, yet the surfer's skillful alignment with the wave's motion determines whether they glide effortlessly or wipe out. Similarly, traders ride market "waves" not by force but by attuning to probability patterns and emotional states, harmonizing intention with flow.

The Philosophy of Non-Attachment

A hallmark of conscious trading is non-attachment to outcomes. This does not imply indifference to profit or loss, but a mindful recognition that outcomes are probabilistic, influenced by countless interconnected factors beyond any single trader's control. Non-attachment fosters:

- **Clarity:** Reduced noise from fear, greed, or frustration.
- **Flexibility:** Ability to adjust strategies without ego interference.
- **Sustainable Performance:** Preserved psychological equilibrium, avoiding burnout or impulsive decision-making.

Integrating Conscious Practices

Conscious trading integrates reflection, mindfulness, and probabilistic reasoning into daily routines. Practical techniques include:

1. **Pre-Trade Alignment:** Brief meditation or focused breathing to center attention and clarify objectives before engaging the market.
2. **Probability Visualization:** Mentally simulating potential market outcomes and corresponding emotional responses.
3. **Post-Trade Reflection:** Analyzing decisions, emotional states, and probabilistic assessments to reinforce learning.
4. **Emotional Calibration Drills:** Practicing real-time labeling, intensity assessment, and behavioral adjustment during live trading.

These practices cultivate a mindset where trading becomes an iterative dance between mind, market, and probability a conscious, adaptive process.

Narrative Insight

An experienced trader recounts a period of consistent losses during high-volatility swings. Initially, the focus was solely on avoiding losses, resulting in reactive decisions dominated by fear. Over time, the trader adopted conscious trading practices: aligning awareness with probabilistic reasoning, practicing emotional calibration, and reflecting on each trade without attachment. Paradoxically, by focusing less on immediate outcomes, both performance and composure improved, illustrating that mastery arises from alignment rather than obsessive control.

Philosophical Reflection

Conscious trading embodies a holistic philosophy: markets are probabilistic ecosystems, and the trader is both participant and observer. By transcending the binary mindset of winning and losing, traders cultivate insight, resilience, and flow. Each trade becomes an opportunity to refine awareness, test hypotheses, and harmonize perception with probability, turning the act of trading into a lifelong practice of learning and self-mastery.

Closing Thoughts

The ultimate value of conscious trading lies beyond financial gain. It is the cultivation of a mind capable of perceiving complexity with clarity, responding adaptively to uncertainty, and sustaining equanimity under pressure. In this framework, profit becomes a byproduct of skillful alignment, while true mastery is measured by the coherence of thought, emotion, and action. By embracing this philosophy, traders transform markets into mirrors for growth, reflection, and the art of living consciously within uncertainty.

Part V

Appendix

Glossary of Key Concepts

This glossary provides clear explanations of the essential concepts used throughout this book. These terms are foundational for understanding probabilistic markets, quantum-inspired decision-making, and conscious trading.

Probability Waves

Probability waves describe the range of potential market outcomes rather than a single deterministic trajectory. Markets are inherently probabilistic; each price point represents a spectrum of possibilities shaped by perception, collective behavior, and external events. **Example:** A stock may have a 40% chance to rise, 50% chance to remain stable, and 10% chance to fall. Visualizing these probabilities as waves helps traders prepare for multiple outcomes.

Superposition

Superposition is the mental ability to hold multiple potential outcomes simultaneously without prematurely committing to any single one. In trading, this encourages flexibility, allowing adaptation as probabilities evolve. **Exercise:** Mentally simulate three possible price movements for an asset and notice your emotional response to each without taking immediate action.

Entanglement

Entanglement refers to the interconnectedness of traders, instruments, and markets. A decision by one market participant can influence correlated assets or other participants, creating complex and non-local interactions. **Analogy:** Like two dancers connected by a tensioned rope, a movement by one affects the other even if they are apart. In markets, this appears as correlated asset behaviors or cascading price effects.

Observer Effect

The observer effect highlights how observation itself influences outcomes. A trader's awareness and decisions alter the probabilistic landscape, emphasizing that perception and action are inseparable from market dynamics. **Example:** Anticipated institutional trades may shift market prices even before execution.

Decoherence

Decoherence occurs when emotional, cognitive, and probabilistic systems fall out of alignment. Distractions, impulsivity, or emotional turbulence can disrupt decision-making, increasing the likelihood of error. **Practice:** Use emotional calibration drills, mindfulness, or focused breathing to restore alignment between awareness and probability perception.

Flow

Flow is a state of deep engagement where awareness, intuition, and action operate harmoniously. In trading, flow is achieved when perception aligns with market probabilities, enabling adaptive and confident decision-making. **Analogy:** A surfer riding a wave intuitively adapts to the water's motion. Similarly, a trader in flow responds to market fluctuations with clarity and precision.

Integration of Concepts

These concepts together provide a framework for quantum-inspired trading. By recognizing probability waves, maintaining superposition, understanding entanglement, accounting for the observer effect, preventing decoherence, and entering flow states, traders cultivate a strategic advantage in probabilistic markets.

Application Exercise

1. Select an asset or market to observe.

2. Identify the probability distribution of possible outcomes (Probability Waves).

3. Mentally hold multiple scenarios without committing (Superposition).

4. Consider correlated instruments or participants that may influence outcomes (Entanglement).

5. Reflect on how your observation might affect your decision (Observer Effect).
6. Assess your emotional and cognitive state; recalibrate if needed (Decoherence).
7. Enter a focused, adaptive decision-making state aligned with market probabilities (Flow).

By integrating these practices, traders develop a conscious, probabilistic mindset, capable of navigating complex markets with clarity, resilience, and adaptability.

Exercises

This appendix provides practical exercises to integrate the concepts of probabilistic markets, conscious decision-making, and flow states. Each exercise is designed to develop mental flexibility, emotional calibration, and adaptive trading skills.

Mental Superposition Practice

Superposition is the ability to hold multiple potential outcomes simultaneously without prematurely committing. Practicing this strengthens cognitive flexibility and prepares traders for uncertainty.

Exercise Steps:

1. Select a financial instrument or market scenario.
2. Identify three to five potential outcomes for price movement (e.g., rise, fall, stable, spike, dip).
3. Visualize each scenario vividly, noting both objective probabilities and subjective impressions.
4. Record emotional responses to each scenario without taking immediate action.
5. Reflect on which scenario you feel most drawn to and why; observe biases.
6. Repeat daily, gradually increasing the number of potential outcomes held in mind.

Probability Visualization Drills

Visualizing probabilities as dynamic waves helps traders anticipate market movements and make informed, adaptive decisions.

Exercise Steps:

1. Draw a simple probability curve for a selected asset, showing likely price ranges and associated probabilities.
2. Mentally animate the curve over time as events unfold (earnings reports, news, market sentiment changes).
3. Observe how your mental probability distribution shifts and adjust your planned trades accordingly.
4. Compare the visualized probabilities with actual market movements and reflect on discrepancies.
5. Practice assigning subjective probabilities to multiple assets simultaneously to train multi-dimensional awareness.

Flow and Attention Alignment Exercises

Flow requires alignment of perception, probability assessment, and action. These exercises cultivate the mental state for conscious, high-probability decision-making under uncertainty.

Exercise Steps:

1. Begin each trading session with a 5–10 minute mindfulness or focused breathing routine to center awareness.
2. Set clear probabilistic intentions: define potential outcomes and probabilities for each trade before execution.
3. During trading, monitor attention and emotional state; use micro-pauses to recalibrate if distraction or emotional spikes occur.
4. After each session, journal flow states: note moments of clarity, distraction, emotional interference, and alignment with probability.
5. Over time, increase session length, complexity of instruments, and number of simultaneous probabilistic assessments to strengthen sustained flow.

Integration Practice

For advanced mastery, combine exercises:

1. Visualize multiple outcomes for several assets (Superposition + Probability Visualization).
2. Maintain mindful awareness and monitor emotions as trades unfold (Flow + Emotional Calibration).
3. Reflect in a journal on alignment, coherence, and adaptive decision-making.

Consistent practice of these exercises develops resilience, clarity, and adaptability key traits for conscious, probabilistic trading mastery.

Case Studies

This chapter explores historical market phenomena through the lens of probabilistic consciousness, highlighting how awareness, probability assessment, and emotional calibration influence trading outcomes. By examining real-world examples, traders can connect conceptual frameworks with practical insights, reinforcing the principles of conscious, probability-driven decision-making.

Historical Market Phenomena via Probabilistic Conscious Frameworks

Understanding historical markets probabilistically allows traders to see beyond deterministic narratives. Each event is not a single outcome but a range of possibilities shaped by collective behavior, perception, and probabilistic alignment.

Example 1: The Dot-Com Bubble (1995–2000)

- **Scenario Analysis:** Probabilities of tech stock growth were inflated by collective optimism, creating high emotional interference (fear of missing out, greed).
- **Observation:** Traders who maintained probabilistic superposition considered potential downturns, assigning non-zero probabilities to crashes despite prevailing bullish sentiment.
- **Reflection:** Superposition and emotional calibration allowed some traders to reduce exposure pre-crash, demonstrating conscious probability weighting in action.
- **Exercise:** Review historical price charts of tech stocks during this period. Assign subjective probabilities to growth, stagnation, and decline at various points, and note emotional biases that could influence these estimates.

Example 2: 2008 Global Financial Crisis

- **Scenario Analysis:** Credit and housing markets exhibited nonlinear feedback loops and entangled decision networks, amplifying systemic risk.
- **Observation:** Traders aligned with probability-based frameworks identified hidden variables and cognitive biases affecting valuation assumptions.
- **Reflection:** Emotional coherence and awareness of interdependence mitigated impulsive decisions, highlighting the importance of observer alignment in complex systems.
- **Exercise:** Construct a probability tree mapping different possible outcomes for mortgage-backed securities. Evaluate how your emotional response might shift probabilities and consider mitigation strategies.

Example 3: 1987 Black Monday Crash

- **Scenario Analysis:** Rapid decoherence in market sentiment led to extreme volatility.
- **Observation:** Traders relying on deterministic models failed to account for probability shifts induced by collective panic.
- **Reflection:** Applying a probabilistic, observer-aware framework would have emphasized multiple outcome monitoring and emotional anchoring, reducing overexposure.
- **Exercise:** Simulate trading positions during high-volatility events using a probabilistic framework. Record potential outcomes and emotional responses to evaluate decision alignment.

Example 4: 2017 Bitcoin Rally

- **Scenario Analysis:** Positive feedback loops and entangled trader networks drove exponential price increases.
- **Observation:** Awareness of cognitive bias (herding and confirmation bias) and use of mental superposition could have helped traders assess risk-reward dynamically and adjust positions intelligently.
- **Reflection:** Integrating flow, attention alignment, and probabilistic decision-making allows traders to participate without being dominated by hype.
- **Exercise:** Create a scenario table with probabilities for Bitcoin or another asset's potential future movements, integrating both market signals and your emotional calibration.

Example 5: Flash Crashes and Microstructure Anomalies

- **Scenario Analysis:** Sub-second anomalies illustrate the need for cognitive alignment with market probabilities and recognition of hidden variables.
- **Observation:** Traders practicing flow and conscious observation are better positioned to react adaptively, integrating short-term volatility into probabilistic decision frameworks.
- **Reflection:** Even milliseconds matter; training awareness and observer alignment creates resilience to unexpected noise.
- **Exercise:** Simulate rapid intraday price movements. Assign probabilities to potential microstructure events and practice making real-time decisions without emotional overreaction.

Analysis of Crashes, Trends, and Anomalies

Market crashes, sustained trends, and anomalies can be understood as probabilistic waves influenced by collective cognition, feedback loops, and emotional currents.

- **Key Insight 1:** Probabilistic frameworks allow traders to prepare for multiple scenarios, rather than expecting deterministic outcomes.
- **Key Insight 2:** Cognitive and emotional coherence allows traders to maintain perspective during extreme events.
- **Key Insight 3:** Observer-aware decision-making and mental superposition provide resilience against reactive behaviors.
- **Key Insight 4:** Historical case analysis combined with practical exercises strengthens probabilistic intuition and emotional calibration for future market events.

Integrative Exercises for Case Studies

1. **Scenario Reimagination:** Select any historical market event. Construct a probability matrix for possible outcomes and overlay your predicted emotional responses at each stage.
2. **Reflection Journaling:** Document decisions you would make under different probabilistic assumptions. Identify potential biases or overconfidence effects.
3. **Feedback Simulation:** Apply adaptive risk management models to historical scenarios, noting how iterative adjustments could change outcome probabilities.

4. **Flow Alignment Exercise:** Mentally simulate market flow states during historical rallies or crashes, focusing on awareness, probability assessment, and emotional coherence.

Conclusion

Analyzing historical markets through the probabilistic conscious framework transforms retrospective observation into actionable learning. By combining conceptual understanding, reflective practice, and scenario-based exercises, traders can integrate awareness, probability, and emotional calibration into their decision-making toolkit. These lessons reinforce that mastery lies not in predicting exact outcomes, but in synchronizing perception, probability, and flow across a dynamic, interconnected market landscape.

References

Academic Sources

1. Kahneman, D. (2011). *Thinking, Fast and Slow.* Farrar, Straus and Giroux.

2. Shiller, R. J. (2015). *Irrational Exuberance.* Princeton University Press.

3. Taleb, N. N. (2007). *The Black Swan: The Impact of the Highly Improbable.* Random House.

4. Mantegna, R. N., & Stanley, H. E. (2000). *An Introduction to Econophysics: Correlations and Complexity in Finance.* Cambridge University Press.

5. Lo, A. W. (2012). *Adaptive Markets: Financial Evolution at the Speed of Thought.* Princeton University Press.

6. Sornette, D. (2003). *Why Stock Markets Crash: Critical Events in Complex Financial Systems.* Princeton University Press.

7. Fama, E. F. (1970). "Efficient Capital Markets: A Review of Theory and Empirical Work." *Journal of Finance*, 25(2), 383–417.

Philosophical and Cognitive Science Sources

1. Bohm, D. (1980). *Wholeness and the Implicate Order.* Routledge.

2. Heisenberg, W. (1958). *Physics and Philosophy: The Revolution in Modern Science.* Harper & Row.

3. James, W. (1890). *The Principles of Psychology.* Henry Holt and Company.

4. Varela, F. J., Thompson, E., & Rosch, E. (1991). *The Embodied Mind: Cognitive Science and Human Experience.* MIT Press.

5. Dennett, D. C. (1991). *Consciousness Explained.* Little, Brown and Co.

6. Kahneman, D., & Tversky, A. (1979). "Prospect Theory: An Analysis of Decision under Risk." *Econometrica*, 47(2), 263–291.

Professional and Trading Sources

1. Elder, A. (2014). *Trading for a Living.* Wiley Trading.
2. Schwager, J. D. (1995). *Market Wizards: Interviews with Top Traders.* Wiley.
3. Tharp, V. K. (2006). *Trade Your Way to Financial Freedom.* McGraw-Hill.
4. Murphy, J. J. (1999). *Technical Analysis of the Financial Markets.* New York Institute of Finance.
5. Mitra, S., & Acharya, R. (2020). *Algorithmic Trading and Quantitative Strategies.* Springer.
6. Chan, E. (2017). *Algorithmic Trading: Winning Strategies and Their Rationale.* Wiley.

Supplementary Sources

1. Taleb, N. N. (2018). *Skin in the Game: Hidden Asymmetries in Daily Life.* Random House.
2. Seligman, M. E. P. (2011). *Flourish: A Visionary New Understanding of Happiness and Well-being.* Free Press.
3. Ariely, D. (2008). *Predictably Irrational: The Hidden Forces That Shape Our Decisions.* HarperCollins.
4. Barabási, A.-L. (2016). *Network Science.* Cambridge University Press.
5. Mlodinow, L. (2008). *The Drunkard's Walk: How Randomness Rules Our Lives.* Pantheon Books.

www.ingramcontent.com/pod-product-compliance
Lightning Source LLC
Chambersburg PA
CBHW050527240926
51846CB00003B/719
* 9 7 8 9 3 3 4 4 5 2 2 6 6 *